PARENTS' GUIDE TO SCHOOL SELECTION

in Alameda/Contra Costa County

Nancy Ginsburg Gill

Haskala Press, Los Altos, California

PARENTS' GUIDE TO SCHOOL SELECTION

in Alameda/Contra Costa County

Published by: Haskala Press
                 640 Orange Ave.
                 Los Altos, CA 94022
                 (415) 948-4648
                 FAX: (415) 941-0567

Production and typesetting by: ASCI
                                  4600 El Camino Real, Ste 203
                                  Los Altos, CA 94022
                                  (415) 948-9477

ISBN: 0-9613846-3-8

TABLE OF CONTENTS

INTRODUCTION

When I was growing up in the old section of Los Altos in the 1950s, the neighborhood children went to either the local public school or a nearby Catholic school. When my husband and I moved back to the same neighborhood in the late 1970s with two children of our own, we discovered that the children living within a three block radius of our home attended twelve different elementary schools — five public and seven private.[*]

In talking with friends and neighbors about schools, I saw how the great increase in school choices, both public and private, had created confusion and often panic among parents who wanted the best for their children. Fears of violence, teacher strikes, budget cuts, and declining academic standards had made parents leery of sending their children to the neighborhood public school. Highly publicized national studies lamenting the state of public education intensified these concerns.

In the winter of 1980, after writing "Choosing a Private School" for *Parents* magazine, I decided to use my experience teaching in public and private schools, the research I had done as an education writer, and my interest in education issues to help parents in Santa Clara and San Mateo Counties through the baffling and often frightening process of finding a school for their children. After four years of working as an education consultant, I wrote the first edition of <u>Parents' Guide to School Selection in Santa Clara and San Mateo County</u>.

When the book came out at the beginning of 1985, I received positive responses from many parents and educators. The fact that both private and public school educators liked what the book had to say made me feel that I had achieved my primary goal: to give parents an unbiased and balanced picture of their school options and offer guidelines that would help them make the best choice for their children.

I used the introductions to the second and third editions of my book to make some general comments about current education issues. When I wrote the first edition, most public school districts were still facing shrinking enrollments. But by the 1990s, many were bursting at the seams in the lower grades; instead of worrying about which schools to close, administrators were wondering how to get funds for new school construction, struggling with the dilemma of needing classroom space that had been rented by day care centers, and trying to cope with the challenge of educating a growing number of ESL — English as a second language — students.

Schools in the nineties are doing a much better job meeting the needs of working parents. In 1984, working mothers often had great difficulty finding

1

---

[*] In this book, for the sake of simplicity, I use the term "private school" to refer to all non-public schools—parochial and private.

schools that provided on-site day care. Now, it is the rare elementary school—private or public—that doesn't have before and after school child care programs; those that don't usually have arrangements with day care centers that bus children to an afterschool facility. However, many working parents still find themselves in a quandary during school holidays as relatively few of these child care facilities stay open year-round.

With the growth of the elementary school population and the retirement of teachers who started teaching in the fifties and sixties, many schools are being infused with the energy of new and returning teachers. Some private schools have felt the negative side of the public school hiring spurt as they have lost good teachers to the higher pay and better benefits offered by public schools; when these schools seek new teachers entering the job market, they now have to compete with the public schools — something they rarely had to do during most of the seventies and the early eighties. Thus, private school tuition has increased substantially over the last decade since these schools can no longer attract and retain good teachers unless they attempt to keep up with the higher salaries paid by the public schools.

California's recession of the early 1990s has affected both public and private schools. Many parents, alarmed by the increased class sizes and program cuts dictated by the state's ongoing budget crisis, have sought a more stable environment in private schools. On the other hand, job insecurity, rising private school tuition, and the prospect of spiraling college costs have sent some private school parents back to the public schools. Furthermore, some parents have discovered that while the big picture for public education in California is grim, many local districts—through the innovations of teachers and administrators, and the utilization of parent volunteers and business and community partnerships—still offer quality education to their students. Also encouraging is that most districts seem to be managing their labor relations better so that teacher strikes are no longer a constant threat as they were a decade ago.

With California's economic recovery, public school educators and parents have hoped that the state would begin increasing the per-pupil funding for its schools, which now ranks 40th among the 50 states. However, with the continuing demands on already-strained state and local budgets, California's public schools are apt to remain underfunded throughout the remainder of the decade.

Many parents and educators are excited by the reforms and innovative programs designed to achieve the goals articulated by the State Department of Education's curriculum frameworks. However, others believe that these reforms—with their emphasis on multicultural education, critical thinking, open-ended questions, heterogeneous grouping, and collaborative learning—ignore the importance of teaching basic skills and will result in the kind of experimental chaos and lowering of standards that drove so many parents into private schools in the seventies and early eighties. Private school admissions officers say that, due to parental concern about the nature of these latest reforms, they are seeing an increasing number of public school applicants. In the summer of 1995, just as this book is going to press, a coalition of

Democratic and Republican state lawmakers has responded to these concerns by sponsoring a bill to mandate instruction in basic skills.

With the publication of the second edition of my book in 1990 and the third edition in 1994, I began to get an increasing number of requests from parents, real estate agents, and relocation specialists for a similar book for the East Bay. A sabbatical from my job as director of Foothill College's Writing Center has provided me the opportunity to write an edition for Alameda and Contra Costa counties .

This book, like those before it, is designed to clarify some of the confusing issues surrounding the public versus private school debate and give parents a better understanding of how to find the best school for their children. After using the directory to identify the schools that will meet their financial, philosophical, and geographical needs, parents should evaluate schools for themselves, using the guidelines provided in the first part of the book. If you make an honest assessment of your child's needs and look for an environment full of enthusiastic, caring educators, chances are your search for the right school for your child will be a successful one.

No established elementary or secondary private school or public school district has been intentionally omitted from this book. Every reasonable effort has been made to see that the listings in the directory are accurate. The publisher and author assume no responsibility for any errors that may have been inadvertently made.

HOW TO START
THE SCHOOL SEARCH

Make an honest assessment of your child's interests, strengths, and weaknesses.
Many children will do well wherever they go. For these families, the school selection process is primarily a matter of finding the school that best meets parental expectations, practical needs, and education values. However, parents should first assess their child's personality, strengths and weaknesses. Some parents feed their own egos and need for status by pushing their children into prestigious schools that may not serve the child's needs at all. No one school is right for all children. A child who is easily distracted might need a structured learning environment, whereas a creative, self-motivated child would flourish in a more open, unstructured school. Children with low self-esteem often need a small school with a low student-to-teacher ratio, a place where they can feel important. More confident children often thrive on the variety and stimulus a large school can offer. Teachers who have worked with your child can be of great help in assessing the class size, amount of structure, and degree of academic pressure that will be best for him or her. If you have difficulty deciding what kind of school will be best for your child, you can also use the services of an education counselor.

Before you start visiting schools, decide what you want in a school.
You will have an easier time evaluating schools if you combine your assessments of your child's specific needs with your own practical requirements (e.g., on site day care, cost, distance from home) and the qualities you think a good school should have. Some parents want structure, discipline, and lots of homework. Others want a more open learning environment, which allows children to learn at their own pace. The better sense you have of what you want in a school, the easier it will be to recognize the right school when you visit it.

You should also decide how involved you want to be in your child's school. Most public schools and some private schools welcome parental involvement in the classroom and on advisory committees. A few public and a growing number of private schools even require participation. Some private schools restrict parent participation to fund-raising efforts and write into their philosophies that volunteer aides are not used in the classroom. Thus, if you have the time and inclination to participate, look for a school that will welcome your involvement.

CONSIDER A PUBLIC SCHOOL

In spite of the many problems facing public education, the San Francisco Bay Area has many excellent public schools. Unless you want a school that offers religious instruction or a special program the public schools can't offer, you would be wise to start your school search by evaluating for yourself the education your child can receive free of charge. Talk to your public school administrators, teachers, and especially parents of current students. By following the "how to evaluate a school" guidelines, you should get a good feeling for the kind of education available in your assigned public school. You may find good teachers and exciting programs. Even if you are not satisfied with the public schools available to you, taking the time to evaluate them will give you a better idea of what you want in a private school.

FUNDING: Several decades ago financing of public education in California was relatively simple but inequitable; it was determined, for the most part, by the assessed value of local property and the extent to which communities were willing to pass local school bonds. However, in 1976, the State Supreme Court ruled in Serrano v. Priest that unequal funding among school districts was unconstitutional. In response to the court order, the Legislature passed a law to redistribute property taxes to reduce inequities. In 1984, the Superior Court declared that sufficient compliance with the Serrano decision had been achieved, and indeed, compared to most other states, there is relatively little disparity in how much tax money each school district receives for each child.

The shift of school finances to state control became virtually complete in 1978 when Proposition 13 capped property taxes. It also limited the ability of local government to add to the state contribution by requiring two-thirds vote to pass local school bonds and parcel taxes.

While Serrano mandated relative equity in what each district receives to educate each child, it did not cover all sources of funding. Many districts and some individual schools, primarily those serving wealthy communities, have established foundations, which in some cases raise hundreds of thousands of dollars annually to hire specialists, buy new textbooks and equipment, and reduce class sizes. Furthermore, seven districts[1] in Alameda and Contra Costa County have been able to win the required two-thirds vote to levy special parcel taxes to raise extra money to improve or maintain instructional programs and/or reduce class size, and seventeen districts[2] have passed general obligation bonds to build, renovate or improve facilities. A district's success at passing such a measure

7

[1] Acalanes, Albany, Berkeley, Lafayette, Moraga, Orinda, Piedmont.
[2] Acalanes, Alameda, Albany, Berkeley, Brentwood, Dublin, Fremont, Liberty Union, Martinez, New Haven, Newark, Oakland, Orinda, Piedmont, Pleasanton, San Ramon Valley, Walnut Creek.

demonstrates broad-based community support for the local public schools. A few very small districts get extra money because they qualify as necessary schools and require extra money per child to run a complete school program.

INTER AND INTRA DISTRICT TRANSFERS. In the summer of 1993, the state legislature passed AB 19 and AB 1114, which allow parents to send their children to any school within their district or in another district as long as space is available. However, if the transfer would have an negative impact on desegregation or if a school has already lost 1 to 3% of its students in a given year, the resident school district can prevent the transfer.

Even before AB 1114 was passed, many districts had an open enrollment policy, allowing parents to choose any school within the district as long as space was available. But by the early 1990s, districts were finding it increasingly difficult to honor these requests, since many schools, especially those deemed "the best," were packed with students from the school's attendance area.

In 1986, the state passed the Allen Bill, which allowed parents to place children in kindergarten through eighth grade in school districts in which their workplace is located. Districts are only required to grant such transfers as long as space is available and as long as such a transfer does not negatively impact a district's desegregation plan or cost the accepting district more money to educate the child than it would receive from the state in additional aid.

Although the Allen Bill, AB 1114 and AB 19 are well-intended efforts to give parents more choice in public schools, they have had little impact. Most school districts are experiencing a population spurt among their own residents and thus are able to grant few transfers under these bills. However, parents who feel their children can receive a better education in another district should inquire about an inter-district transfer as provided by these bills.

Magnet Schools are used by some large school districts to help balance the student ethnic distribution of the district's schools. These schools emphasize one of a wide variety of areas such as performing arts and computer science and integrate the specialty throughout the school's curriculum.

Alternative Schools. Many districts also operate alternative schools that have a different focus or philosophy than the neighborhood schools. If your district does offer such schools, start investigating them as soon as possible because these schools often have long waiting lists.

Back-to-Basics Schools generally have a teacher-directed, textbook approach to learning with a minimum amount of individualization. They often have a dress code and clearly defined homework and discipline policies. Grade levels are rarely combined, and parents are generally not used as classroom aides. Students and parents are often required to sign a written agreement to follow the rules and philosophy of the school. These schools appeal to parents who want a traditional, highly structured program for their children. They are especially effective for children who need firm guidelines and a quiet environment. Very bright or creative children sometimes find the structure and textbook orientation of these schools too confining.

Open Education Schools are characterized by student initiated activity, independent study, and freedom of movement in the classroom. Open schools are less textbook oriented than most schools and instead emphasize an inter-disciplinary and hands-on approach to learning. These schools often mix age groups and may require parent participation to achieve the low student-to-adult ratio necessary for individualized education. Open schools usually do not give graded report cards, but instead evaluate students through written comments and conferences. Open schools generally work best for creative, self-motivated children who thrive on freedom of choice, and they appeal to parents who want to be actively involved in their children's education. They are not appropriate for children who are easily distracted, who are overwhelmed by too many choices, or who have learning styles that require systematic and sequential instruction to grasp basic skills.

(Note: Most public schools belong in the middle of the educational spectrum between open schools and back-to-basics schools. In the 1970s many schools moved towards the open end of the spectrum; in the early 1980s, many public schools moved back towards a more structured model. In recent years, the emphasis on "school reform" and the desire to implement the goals articulated by California's curriculum frameworks have led many schools to embrace some of the ideas—e.g., integrated curriculum, collaborative learning, mixed age grouping— that typify "open" schools and were a part of the reform movements twenty-five years ago. But now, as this book goes to press, state lawmakers have proposed legislation that would require schools to put more emphasis on basic skills. All of this illustrates what is referred to as "the pendulum swing" in public education.)

Charter Schools. Under new legislation (SB 1448), California allows school districts to abandon the 11-volume, 7,800 Education Code and create whatever kind of school the community wants, as long as its curriculum meets basic state education requirements. Thus far, no charter school has been established in Alameda or Contra Costa County.

Continuation Schools. Almost every high school district offers a continuation program designed for students who have difficulty adjusting to regular school programs, who fail to attend classes according to district criteria, or who have already dropped out of the regular high school. These schools' academic programs are often individualized according to students' needs, and the student-to-teacher ratio is lower than that of the comprehensive high school. Some districts also offer Opportunity Programs directed at middle school students who have been evaluated as potential drop-outs. An increasing number of districts are implementing other programs to identify potential drop-outs and offer specialized programs to motivate these students to stay in school.

Year-Round Schools: Over the last two decades, an increasing number of districts have started operating year-round schools. Students in these schools attend school the same number of days (about 180) as children in schools with traditional calendars, but instead of a three month summer break, vacation and

9

instructional periods are spread more evenly throughout the year, e.g., 60 days of instruction followed by 20 days of vacation. When year-round schools are single-track, all students are in school at the same time. Multi-track schools divide the students and staff into three to five tracks, so that one track is always on vacation. This system allows districts to save on school construction costs as each school site can serve 20% or more students.

Proponents of year-round schools argue that eliminating the obsolete, traditional school calendar improves academic achievement; reduces teacher, student, and parent burn-out; and makes more efficient use of school facilities. However, the implementation of year-round schools has not spread as quickly as many had predicted because it can cause inconvenience to parents with children on different school calendars and because operating schools throughout the summer months requires many districts to install air-conditioning, an expense few can afford. Relatively few high schools have changed to a year-round schedule because of logistical problems (e.g., running athletic programs when students and other schools are on different calendars) and because many high school students rely on summer jobs to help them save money for college.

Education for Children with Disabilities. Every public school district provides special education programs for students with disabilities. Resource specialist programs (RSPs) serve students who qualify for special education services but are able to spend most of the school day in regular classrooms. Specialists provide individual and small group instruction, conduct educational assessments, and coordinate the child's educational program with classroom teachers and parents. School districts also offer, either within the district or in cooperation with other districts, special day classes for students whose learning style make it difficult for them to keep up with regular classroom work. School districts and the County Offices of Education also offer other programs for the more severely disabled.

Under federal and state laws, public funding can be used to pay for sending children with disabilities to specialized private schools. These laws state that if a resident school district does not provide an appropriate program for a disabled child, that child may be funded at a non-public institution, which has been certified by the California State Department of Education and can appropriately meet the needs of the student. For more information on these laws, inquire at your public school district, the State Department of Education, or contact the **Community Alliance for Special Education (CASE)** at its Hayward office (510) 783-5333. CASE offers free consultations about special education rights and services. It also provides legal support, representation, and educational consulting to parents whose children need special education services.

The Parents' Educational Resource Center (415-513-0920) in San Mateo provides information for parents of students with learning differences. Resources include a special library, information/referral services, educational programs, guidance, and a parent newsletter. PERC has opened an East Bay library, which contains a collection of its most popular materials. The library is located at the Ann Martin Children's Center on Grand Ave. near the Oakland-Piedmont border. To schedule appointments to use the library or to meet with the Learning Director, call Nauma Peiser, M.A., at (510) 655-7880, ext. 70.

Gifted and Talented Education Program (GATE) is a state-funded program designed to offer special instruction to children identified as mentally gifted or talented. In the early 1980s, 50% or more of the students in some districts qualified for the program because they tested above a designated score — usually 132 — on intelligence tests. However, the funding is now based on a statewide average which covers a lower percentage of the school population and may vary each year. Most districts, especially those with large numbers of high-testing children, have tightened the criteria for placement in GATE, and the method used to identify these students varies greatly from district to district. Most often districts use a combination of teacher or counselor recommendations, performance on intelligence tests, and demonstrated potential in leadership or performance art to identify children they think need more stimulation and challenge than they are receiving in the classroom. Increasing numbers of educators advocate integrating GATE programs into the regular classroom for they believe that all students deserve the kind of stimulating, enriching activities that typify instruction for the gifted.

The specific programs offered to GATE students vary from district to district. Most often, students are pulled out of their regular classrooms once or twice a week and given special instruction. Some districts use GATE funds to hire specialists to help the classroom teachers keep their exceptional students challenged. A few districts offer cluster programs, in which gifted students are placed together in self-contained classes designed to meet the needs of especially bright students. Once students reach junior high or middle school, clustering of gifted children occurs more naturally, as these children tend to be the ones taking foreign languages and advanced math and science classes. In high school, this natural clustering of the gifted increases as bright students — at least the academically motivated ones — group together in honors classes and the most challenging college preparatory classes. A growing number of community colleges and universities also offer programs designed for gifted elementary and secondary students.

Many advocates for gifted children are concerned that the current emphasis on heterogeneous grouping and collaborative learning, while perhaps beneficial to low achieving and average children, is detrimental to exceptionally bright and motivated students. If you have such a child and are considering a high school or middle school that has eliminated or de-emphasized ability grouping, you should investigate whether the curriculum adequately challenges all students.

The California Association of the Gifted (C.A.G.) is an advocacy and information organization for teachers and parents of gifted children. For information, write C.A.G., 426 Escuela, Suite 19, Mountain View, CA 94040 or phone (415)965-0653.

LOOK INTO THE HEALTH OF YOUR PUBLIC SCHOOL DISTRICT.
Learn how well the components of your public school district work by reading local newspaper coverage of school board meetings and attending some meetings. Try to answer the following questions: Do board members work well together for the good of the schools and the children, or are factions on the school board working against each other? Are teachers constantly threatening to go on strike? Do they seem distrustful of the administration and school board? Are teachers, administrators, parents, and the board working together to solve problems and improve the schools? Are parents and teachers given the opportunity to offer input when difficult decisions must be made regarding the future of the schools? Do constant accusations and bickering characterize the communication level within the school community, or is there a feeling of mutual respect? Have administrators and teachers in your district improved the educational programs in their schools through joint ventures with local businesses and grants from private foundations?

WARNING TO NEWCOMERS: If you are buying or renting a home specifically because you like a certain school in that neighborhood or like the idea of living close to your child's school, don't assume that the Realtor is correct when she or he tells you what school your child will attend. Check with the school district to make sure that your child will be able to attend that school. Some newcomers have been told that the only school with space for their children is across town or have discovered that the house they have bought is not in the school district they thought they were moving into. To save yourself this kind of disappointment and frustration, contact the school district before you commit to a house or apartment.

CONDUCTING A PRIVATE SCHOOL SEARCH

One advantage private schools have over public institutions is that they don't have to be all things to all people. A private school can say, "These are our objectives, these are the methods we use to reach them, and these are the kinds of children we want to educate. If this is what you want and your child meets our qualifications, you are welcome to apply. Otherwise, go elsewhere." Therefore, parents searching for a private school should take special care in evaluating their child's needs and their own educational values.

As readers might notice when reading through the private school directory, school philosophies often sound very similar: "We offer a sound academic program while we develop in our students responsibility, self-confidence, and a concern for others." Visiting the school and talking with parents will help you determine whether you are comfortable with the environment and methods a school uses to achieve its goals. While some schools might work toward responsibility and academic excellence by offering a structured classroom environment and stressing homework, other schools seek to achieve the same goals by giving students the freedom to explore areas of study that interest them.

INQUIRE ABOUT THE CREDENTIALS AND BACKGROUNDS OF THE FACULTY. While many private schools hire only credentialed teachers, some do not. However, parents should not select a school purely on this basis. Many weak teachers have credentials; many excellent ones do not. Some private schools, especially secondary ones, look for staff with a variety of skills, advanced degrees, and practical experience in their subject matter, and consider the possession of a credential relatively unimportant. However, parents considering a school that does not require teaching credentials should carefully assess the caliber of teaching through parent and student evaluations and, if possible, class visitations. Beware of schools staffed almost completely by young, inexperienced teachers.

CHECK THE FACULTY TURNOVER RATE. Although salaries at private schools are usually lower than those at public schools, private schools generally pride themselves on having dedicated, hard-working teachers. Up until the mid-1980s, young teachers in this area found that the only job opportunities were in private schools as shrinking enrollments and budget cuts brought public school hiring virtually to a halt. However, now that public schools are experiencing growing enrollment and many veteran teachers are retiring, capable young teachers and returning teachers have many more job choices. Although most private schools can't compete with public school salaries and benefits, many teachers who could get public school jobs stay on at good private schools for a number of reasons: small classes, close personal relationships with students, a minimum of disciplinary problems and bureaucratic red-tape, more control over curriculum, or in the case of religious schools, the opportunity to teach in a religious environment. A high teacher turn-over rate at a private school may indicate that a school does not offer enough of these advantages or that the salaries are dismally low.

CHECK ON THE SCHOOL'S FINANCIAL SOLVENCY. Few private schools can operate on tuition revenue alone. Most parochial schools are subsidized by their supporting church and therefore can offer private education at a relatively low cost to parents. Older schools often have substantial endowment funds and annual alumni fund-raising drives. Many schools rely on parents' fund-raising efforts to pay for special programs, scholarships and improvements. Almost all private schools publish some sort of annual financial report. If you are concerned about a school's financial solvency, do not be afraid to ask to read this report.

Proprietary schools operate under private ownership as profit-making ventures. Consequently, they cannot qualify for tax-exempt donations and must pay property taxes. Some educators are skeptical of any school run on such a basis. However, many proprietary schools are operated by dedicated educators and provide excellent programs. If you are interested in a proprietary school, check carefully to determine whether the school provides necessary services and materials to its students, sufficiently small classes, and adequate salaries to maintain a strong faculty while still making a profit for its owner.

UNDERSTAND THE DIFFERENCES IN PRIVATE SCHOOLS.
Carden Schools were started in the 1930s in New York City by Mae Carden and soon spread throughout the country. The curriculum is highly organized and stresses continuity from grade to grade. Reading, language and grammar instruction begin in kindergarten. The textbooks are privately printed and designed so that skills are taught in clear sequence. Emphasis on written and oral communication in a structured environment characterizes Carden schools. Carden teachers do not have to be credentialed by the state, but they must go through special Carden training and attend instructional seminars twice a year. Each Carden school runs independently — some as non-profit and some as proprietary institutions — but all must be accredited by the Carden Foundation. The degree of academic acceleration varies from school to school, depending on the abilities of the school's students.

Christian Schools. The label "Christian School" applies to schools that have an evangelical or fundamentalist approach to theology and integrate the Bible in almost all aspects of the school curriculum. Most are operated by churches which adhere to a literal interpretation of the Bible, but only a few require that students' families belong to a specific church. Christian schools usually use *A Beka* or other Christian texts; most use them along with secular textbooks, but some use these materials exclusively. Many of these schools offer specialized programs for students with learning disabilities. (Note: Some schools with Christian church affiliations are not considered "Christian Schools" in the above sense because they do not take an evangelical approach to religion, and they teach academic subjects in a secular manner.)

Day-Care Originated Private Schools. In the last two decades, there has been a great increase in the number of schools that started out originally as preschool/day care centers and have responded to working parents' needs by expanding into elementary programs. These schools are generally owner-operated, stay open year-round, and include extended day care as part of the tuition. These schools vary greatly in quality and philosophy.

Independent School is a term generally used for non-church affiliated, non-profit private schools, but some schools that belong to the National Association of Independent Schools (NAIS) and the California Association of Independent Schools (CAIS) do have religious affiliations. While independent schools may include the teaching of religious values and traditions in their philosophy, they teach academic subjects with a secular approach.

Independent schools tend to be more expensive than other private schools but usually have much smaller class sizes and are generally generous with financial aid. They are governed by boards of trustees and usually list preparation for high school or college as their primary goal. Because they are independent, these schools vary greatly in philosophy, structure, and academic programs.

Montessori Schools. In the early 1900s Maria Montessori, an Italian physician and educator, developed her ideas on education from observing slum children in Rome. Her belief that children have a great capacity for mental concentration, a desire to repeat activities, and a love of order led her to write influential books on education, which formed the basis for the Montessori method. Montessori schools stress the importance of a rich environment to provide children the opportunity to understand the world through sensory experiences. The Montessori teacher generally keeps a low profile, allowing children to move from one set of carefully designed materials to another as they wish. Montessori education stresses self-motivated learning and strives to develop self-discipline and self-confidence. Because any school can use Montessori in its title, "Montessori" schools vary greatly in quality and approach.

Roman Catholic Schools are committed to teaching the principles of the Roman Catholic Church while offering a strong academic program. However, Catholic schools can vary in their educational philosophy, structure, and overall flavor. Some are highly structured and traditional; others are more relaxed, open, and innovative. Catholic schools often use state-adopted texts, and usually educate the same spectrum of children as are found in public schools. While most

Catholic schools do not feel equipped to educate seriously handicapped children, some offer programs for those with mild learning disabilities.

Most Catholic elementary schools are parish (parochial) schools operated under the sponsorship of a specific church. Tuition at these schools is relatively low compared to the fees charged by other non-public schools, and the tuition discounts for siblings are substantial. A few secondary schools are operated by religious orders. These non-parochial Catholic schools are usually more expensive than parish schools but tend to have smaller class sizes.

All Catholic schools give admissions priority to qualified Catholic applicants. They welcome non-Catholic students when space is available but expect all students to participate in the school's religious instruction.

Waldorf Schools, started in Germany in 1919 by Rudolf Steiner, stress the relationship between the physical, psychological, and the spiritual. Steiner believed that children pass through distinct·stages of development, and the Waldorf curriculum and teaching methods reflect these separate stages. In Waldorf schools, the class teachers continue from grade to grade with the same children and are responsible for their main subjects. Other teachers teach foreign languages, music, eurythmy (movement), crafts and games. Waldorf Schools do not use traditional textbooks in the early grades; instead the curriculum relies on oral presentations by the teachers and lesson books created by the children for each subject studied. Administrative decisions are made collectively by the faculty who work from consensus.

Other Schools. Some private schools listed in this book do not fall into any of the above categories. Most of these are either proprietary schools (see explanation on page 14) or are affiliated with a particular religion, e.g., Jewish, Episcopal, Islamic, Seventh Day Adventist. Parents can learn about the philosophy and curriculum of these schools by reading the entries listed in the directory and contacting the schools.

HOW TO EVALUATE A SCHOOL

ASSESS THE LEADERSHIP QUALITIES OF THE PRINCIPAL (called the director, headmaster, or headmistress at many private schools.) Your child's education will certainly be shaped largely by the quality of individual teachers; however, a strong principal can create an atmosphere that inspires staff members to put more energy into their jobs and fosters the high morale and family feeling that creates a sense of community among teachers, parents, and students. To assess the quality of leadership in a school, talk to parents, students, and teachers, and, if possible, arrange a meeting with the principal to help you answer some of the following questions:

- Do parents feel comfortable telephoning the principal when a problem arises that teachers cannot or will not handle? Are calls returned and, when necessary, conferences arranged?

- Does the principal support the staff, but still respond to legitimate complaints when parents feel teachers are not doing their jobs?

- Does the principal take the time to know the students? Does he or she make appearances on the playground, in the lunch area, and in classrooms, and participate in activities with students?

- Do students and teachers respect but not fear or hate the principal?

- Can the principal clearly describe the school's curriculum, and is he or she excited about the school's programs?

- When discipline problems arise in the classroom or on the playground, does the principal respond immediately and effectively?

If you get an affirmative answer to all or most of these questions, then you have found a place with one of the most important elements of a healthy school — strong leadership.

EVALUATE THE TEACHERS. In evaluating the quality of teaching at any school, parents should realize that no one teacher is perfect for all children and that no one school has only "star" teachers. Some children do best with hard-nosed disciplinarians who stretch students with demanding assignments and run a "tight ship" in the classroom. Others wilt under pressure and are happier and more productive with warmer, more nurturing teachers.

A lot of your information will come from talking with parents, but you should remember that tastes in teachers can be like tastes in movies — the reviews can be so different that you will wonder if people are talking about the same person. Unfortunately, many schools have at least one or two "lemons" — teachers who, according to almost everyone, are incompetent, burned-out, or just plain mean or indifferent. Schools usually also have at least as many "stars" — teachers whom parents and students praise for their extraordinary teaching abilities. Avoid schools that have a large number of "lemons" and look for one that has at least one or two "stars."

Class visits can help you judge the caliber of teaching at a school. Most public schools and some private schools welcome such visits as long as prior arrangements are made with the school office. Do not judge too harshly schools that do not allow such visits. Some schools, especially large private ones with many applicants, consider class visitations disruptive and logistically impossible. If a school does not allow classroom observation, ask to attend an open house or back-to-school night. Such a visit may give you an opportunity to talk to teachers or at least hear about and see the results of what goes on in the classroom.

Through classroom visits, attendance at open house, and discussions with parents and current students, try to answer the following questions:

- Do teachers explain material clearly and respond to questions without putting down students?

- Is the degree of discipline and control in the classroom what you want for your child? If you want a structured classroom, be sure that control is not achieved through fear or intimidation. If you want an open learning environment, be sure that freedom does not result in chaos.

- Do teachers discipline children without cruelty or sarcasm?

- Do teachers seem to enjoy their jobs and bring energy, enthusiasm, and empathy into the classroom?

- Are teachers willing to spend extra time — recess, lunch, or afterschool time if necessary — to explain material a child did not understand in class?

- Do teachers clarify class rules and the consequences of breaking the rules and follow through with consistency and fairness?

- Do teachers combine solid instruction in basic skills with projects and study units that generate excitement and intellectual curiosity? Even if you are primarily interested in a "basics" school, do not forget that stimulation of intellectual curiosity is probably the most important element of a good education. Ask parents if their children ever come home excited about what they are learning. When visiting classrooms, do you see only math dittoes and spelling tests covering the walls? Or is there evidence of more interesting assignments as well — creative writing samples, social studies projects, and science experiments?

You will probably never find a school where every teacher is wonderful, and it would probably be impossible to answer all of the above questions for every member of a school's faculty. But talking to members of the school community and spending time at the school should give you a good sense of how enthusiastic, caring, and competent a school's teachers are.

LOOK AT THE CURRICULUM. Asking questions and making observations about curriculum can also help determine whether a school will meet your expectations and be appropriate to your child's needs.

- Are the textbooks up-to-date?

- Is there a healthy balance between development of basic skills and the exploration of ideas and thinking skills?

- What ability level is the school geared toward? (This question is especially important if the school stresses group instruction as part of its philosophy.) If your child seems to fall above or below the ability norm of the general student body, ask how ability levels are handled. Are brighter children allowed to move ahead at a faster pace and given more challenging assignments? Or are they merely given 40 math problems instead of the normal 20 to keep them busy? Are slower students given extra help and more time to grasp concepts and complete work?

In specific areas, consider the following:

Reading. For decades, educators have debated the best approach to teaching reading. While the terminology has changed over the years, the issue is generally the same: proponents of phonics believe children should first learn the letters and the sounds the letters make so that they can decode words and learn to spell correctly. Advocates of what is now termed the "whole language approach" argue that the tedious drill and repetition of phonics instruction kills off enthusiasm for reading, and that children should be allowed to learn to read and write through the desire to express and understand what is important to them. Instead of beginning with the individual letters and sounds, the whole language approach de-emphasizes correct spelling and de-coding in the early years and instead concentrates on the "whole." Sounds are taught through rhythm, repetition and context. Critics of this approach argue that it doesn't give students the basic phonic skills needed to spell accurately and sound out unfamiliar words. Most good teachers recognize the value of generating enthusiasm and interest in reading by exposing students to exciting literature at an early age, but at the same time know the importance of emphasizing, through multi-sensory techniques, the relationships of sounds and letters. Avoid primary grade teachers who are dogmatic about "the one" best approach to teach reading.

At the elementary level, look for schools that use a mixture of materials and techniques to stimulate interest in reading. Literature assignments, oral reading by the teacher and students, and regular outside reading assignments should be used instead of or in combination with traditional reading textbooks. Many schools—public and private—set aside a specific time of day for school-wide silent, sustained reading to promote the concept that reading is a relaxing, enjoyable experience.

At the secondary level, an examination of required reading lists and syllabuses will help you determine whether the school's curriculum is appropriate to your child's abilities and your values and expectations. While a few secondary schools still pride themselves on assigning only "classics" —e.g., Shakespeare, Dickens, Hawthorne—most are committed to a multicultural approach that reflects the rich diversity of our population and history. Whatever a school's philosophy about literature, the English classes should generate enthusiasm for reading and promote the ability to discuss and write about literature beyond the purely literal level of book reports.

Math. Of all the areas of the curriculum, changes in math instruction have probably generated the most controversy in recent years. With the accessibility of the calculator and the demands of the modern workplace for employees who can analyze and think independently, many math classes have changed their focus. Instead of merely asking students to show their work and arrive at "the correct answer," teachers of what some call "the new, new math" expect students to be able to apply their math skills to real life situations, teach that there are usually numerous ways to solve a problem, and ask students to be able to explain how they arrive at solutions. This new approach to math is often taught in classrooms in which much of the instructional time is spent with students working in groups of mixed abilities. Some parents and math traditionalists are concerned that the "new new math" slights instruction in basic math skills and that the use of collaborative learning and heterogeneous grouping will hold back the more advanced students and frustrate the slower students.

The debate over how math should best be taught will probably continue for years, but parents would be wise to investigate how teachers feel about the classes they teach. If they are properly trained and enthusiastic about what they are doing and the students seem to be positive about their math instruction, the math program is probably an effective one.

Whether or not a school is traditional, math programs in the early primary grades should use manipulative materials to emphasize an understanding of concepts. Beware of schools that rely almost completely on rote learning of number facts without stressing mathematical concepts. Also look for programs that stress problem solving, logic, and real-life applicability without ignoring the importance of learning number facts and being able to do basic computation.

Up until a few years ago, most middle and high schools tracked their math classes. Students with strong math skills were placed in Algebra I in the eighth or even seventh grade and moved through Calculus by the end of senior year. Those who performed poorly on math placement tests remained in basic math classes, for it was assumed that they could not pass Algebra I or Geometry. In recent years, with the swing towards heterogeneous grouping, and the concern that too many students were being stigmatized as failures before they even entered high school, many schools are now committed to making certain that every student take Algebra. Unfortunately, many schools still assign their weakest math teachers to the weakest students and reward their "star" teachers with the accelerated classes. If you have a child who struggles with math, ask parents as well as administrators about the school's policy regarding this issue. If you have a child entering high school who is exceptionally gifted at math, find out how far a school can take him or her and whether the school has provisions for students to take advanced classes at a local community college or university.

Spelling. Spelling, like math, has become increasingly controversial in the past year. To encourage children to want to write and to express themselves freely, many public and private elementary schools have de-emphasized the importance of correct spelling in the primary grades. Proponents of what many call "creative spelling" argue that this technique works because children who love to write will want to learn to spell words correctly and will improve their spelling as they progress through school. They believe that just as we shouldn't criticize the pronunciation and grammar of toddlers learning to talk, we shouldn't dampen young students' eagerness to write by pointing out all their mistakes.

Critics of this approach argue that children who are praised for essays rife with misspellings are taught that correct spelling is unimportant. They also believe that the absence of traditional spelling books and drill in the curriculum means that many students never learn basic spelling rules and never memorize the irregular spellings of many commonly used words. Look for teachers who are able to generate enthusiasm for writing while at the same time use a variety of techniques to help their students become good spellers.

Composition. Look for a school that has defined expectations in the quantity and quality of writing it expects from students. A good writing program not only stresses the mechanics required for clear expression but also teaches the process of how to write, exposes students to different kinds of writing, and inspires students to want to write. Beware of programs at either the elementary or secondary level that focus almost completely on grammar, spelling and sentence diagramming with little emphasis on actual composition. When evaluating secondary schools, ask parents and students how much writing is assigned, whether the assignments require higher level thinking skills than mere book reports, and if compositions are returned with meaningful teacher comments.

Science. Recognizing that most classroom elementary school teachers were not science majors, many private schools and a few public school districts hire science specialists to enrich the science curriculum. A good science program gives children the opportunity to observe, experiment, and use problem-solving techniques—in other words to experience the methods and tools that scientists use. A purely textbook approach to science—especially one that emphasizes memorizing facts—at either the elementary or secondary level, is one of the surest ways to stifle a child's natural curiosity about the world. The best high school science programs are those that prepare advanced students to do well on the Advanced Placement tests while still maintaining for all students the exciting sense of discovery that comes from well-designed lab work. Also look for programs that demonstrate to students that understanding modern science and all the ethical dilemmas it presents is of increasing importance to all of us, no matter what field we enter. A growing number of high schools are offering integrated science courses that combine life, physical and earth science. However, if your child aspires to continue on at a competitive private college or a UC campus, make sure that the science courses he or she takes fulfill the entrance requirements for those schools.

Computer education. In the 1970s and 1980s, many schools enthusiastically invested in computers and then discovered that their teachers didn't really know what to do with them. Furthermore, much of the early educational software was disappointing as it was primarily limited to games and computerized workbooks and drills. In the last few years, educators have begun to realize the extent to which technology can revolutionize the classroom. The quality of software has improved, and many more teachers have attended computer workshops and even developed their own programs. Furthermore, with the advent of interactive computer programs, schools that have invested in computer technology are finding exciting new ways to engage even "reluctant" learners, stimulate critical thinking and create successful collaborative learning experiences. By plugging into the information highway, educators can break the isolation of the classroom as students communicate with other students across the globe and bring the resources of libraries and museums into the classroom.

Unfortunately, keeping up with the computer revolution is a costly endeavor. Along with the expense of the hardware and software, comes the added expense of training teachers to make best use of the technology and the often daunting challenge of rewiring school plants that were built decades ago. Some educators and parents argue that the money required to establish a model technology program is not worth sacrificing other areas that make up a quality education, e.g., small classes and a strong arts program. Others are concerned that many of today's children are already overly "plugged in" to computers and T.V.'s at home and contend that schools need to focus on the human element of the classroom as the dominant instructional medium.

If a school appeals to you because it offers "computer education" and "computers in the classroom," you would be wise to investigate the degree of enthusiasm teachers express for using computers as an educational tool and the ability of the staff or district advisors to select high-quality software which enhances the quality of instruction throughout the curriculum.

Social studies and history. By the time children complete the sixth grade, they should have a strong background in key events in American history, a respect for other cultures, and familiarity with world geography. Look for schools that teach these basic areas while generating interest in the subject matter through assigning historical fiction and using non-textbook activities like special projects, simulation games, interactive computer software, field trips, movies (but beware of teachers who rely too much on movies to keep students entertained), guest speakers, and research papers.

At the secondary level, history classes should not be merely exercises in regurgitation. Look for programs that emphasize thinking, study, and research skills. A good history class should also include essay questions on exams. Also look for schools that have realized the value of coordinating English and history instruction so that while students are studying American history, they are also reading American literature of the period.

The Arts. Some parents consider a strong arts program merely a frill; others view the arts as an essential part of a good education. If you are one of the latter, certainly ask about a school's art, music, and drama programs. When public school districts were hit by the budget crunch of the 1970s, many of the first cutbacks came in the arts curriculum. Instrumental and choral music teachers found their jobs cut or completely eliminated, and art specialists were relegated to volunteer status. In fact, many districts have come to rely on volunteer help using music and art volunteer docents to run programs formerly taught by paid specialists. These docent-run programs are often excellent, but many districts don't have a stable group of non-working parents to volunteer their time for the programs. Some elementary schools are blessed with classroom teachers who have a strong background in the arts, and thus, despite a shortage of art docents and the lack of funds to pay specialists, their students continue to get enriched exposure to the fine arts. Some innovative districts have won grants from the California Arts Commission to establish artists-in-residence programs which bring working artists to the schools to offer art education to both students and teachers.

Many private schools hire part or full time specialists to teach art, music, and drama. (In fact, having these specialists is often a draw that keeps teachers who aren't comfortable teaching this part of the curriculum in private schools. They are willing to work for lower pay, knowing they won't be responsible for teaching all aspects of their students' education.)

Often in high schools — both public and private — the success of a specific arts program is determined by a single individual. For example, on the San Francisco Peninsula, one public high school has an extraordinary chorus, another a nationally known jazz band, and another an award winning marching band. One private school has an exceptionally strong public speaking program, another has an outstanding drama department, and a third has an excellent visual arts program. All of these programs are generated by the energy, enthusiasm, and expertise of one specific teacher. If your child has demonstrated talent or interest in a specific area of the arts, look for a school known for its strength in that area. Educators have long understood that students who are involved in extracurricular activities are far more likely to have a positive high school experience.

EVALUATE THE SCHOOL ENVIRONMENT. Walking around a campus during school hours can be a helpful way of determining whether you will be happy with a school. Take note of the following:

Recess and lunch periods. Are recesses well supervised? Do children wander around aimlessly, or do most seem involved in games and playground activities? Are playground fights very common, and when they do occur, are they handled effectively? Do children toss litter around, or do they show a sense of pride in their school by using trash cans? Are the restrooms clean? Is there graffiti on the walls? Do children seem relaxed and happy?

The library. If a school has a library, is there a professional librarian, an aide, or a parent volunteer? Does this person have the warmth and enthusiasm that makes students want to use the library and seek out that person's advice? Do students treat the library with respect? Is there evidence on the bulletin boards and walls of staff efforts to stimulate students' interest in reading? Are the books current, and is the collection appropriate to the size and age level of the student body? Is the library automated so that the school research capabilities are greatly expanded beyond its own collection of materials, and do those who staff the library patiently explain to students how to make use of the computers? If a school cannot afford a librarian, a well-stocked library, or computers—and some good ones cannot—ask how the school stimulates interest in reading and teaches research skills.

The sounds of a school. When you walk by classrooms, is the dominant sound a teacher yelling at unruly students, or do you hear encouragement, lively class discussions, and occasional laughter. Do students speak to each other with kindness or with teasing and cruelty? Whether you want a highly structured school, an open one, or something in between, look for a school that makes learning a joyful experience in a calm atmosphere.

SPECIAL THINGS TO CONSIDER WHEN LOOKING FOR AN ELEMENTARY SCHOOL.

- If you need all day care for your child, closely examine what the before and after school activities involve.

  Parents should be certain that the school's child care program doesn't just mean sitting children down in front of a television set or turning them loose on a playground with minimal supervision. Look for a program that provides enriching activities provided by a trained, enthusiastic, and *stable* staff. Some child care operations pay employees so little that there is a constant turn-over of employees.

- If you are thinking of sending your child to a school some distance from your home, consider your child's social needs and your own sanity.

  In their zeal to give their children the best education, parents sometimes forget to include neighborhood friends as an important factor in the school selection process. If you do choose a school far from home and there aren't many other children in your area attending the school, sign your child up for neighborhood athletic teams or scout troops to give him or her the opportunity to make friends to play with during weekends and vacations. Furthermore, don't commit yourself to long drives unless you can do so without disrupting your home and work life, and you are confident that the stress of a long school commute won't adversely affect you or your child.

- Ask about a school's homework policy and consider whether it matches your needs and your child's abilities.

  If you want evening and weekend time to spend on family activities, a school that gives several hours of homework a night might be inappropriate. Inquire about the nature as well as the quantity of homework. Homework is useful if it broadens a child's interest in and understanding of classwork while developing good study habits. It is meaningless and potentially damaging if it is merely busy work or if the quantity is inappropriate to the age and ability of the child.

THINGS TO CONSIDER WHEN CHOOSING A MIDDLE SCHOOL.
In recent years, educators have paid increasing attention to students in the preteen and early teenage years and the schools that serve these students. Formerly, these students were typically placed in junior high schools which treated the students as if they were just smaller versions of high school students. In 1986, a California study group issued a report that defined sixth, seventh and eighth grades as the "neglected grades." The concerns and recommendations of this group were echoed in the spring of 1989 in the Carnegie report on the Education of Young Adolescents. This report pointed out that "the guidance they [students] needed as children and need no less as adolescents is withdrawn" just as pressures to try drugs, alcohol, and early sex intensify. Parents evaluating schools for this age-group should look for schools which have in place programs recommended by these study groups — programs which:

- de-emphasize rote skills and encourage critical and analytical thinking
- provide block scheduling or schools within schools to ensure that all students feel part of a community of teachers and students
- offer classes in health education.

Since private school programs for this age group are typically small, early adolescents at these schools usually do not experience the kind of anonymous, impersonal treatment typical of large public junior highs. However, some K-gr. 8 private schools have difficulty keeping their students for the sixth, seventh, and eighth grade years. Many private school families, even some who plan to send their children to private high schools, switch to public middle schools — sometimes because the children themselves want the "rite of passage" experience of going to a new, bigger school that can offer more electives, social choices, and athletic opportunities.

In choosing a middle school, parents should consider their child's needs and personality. Confident children may love the novelty and stimulus of a large school that offers a full spectrum of electives, extensive athletic and extracurricular programs, and a broad range of social choices. Others may continue to need the security of knowing the principal and most of their classmates and teachers. However, parents should also note that a very small middle-school can be socially difficult for some children. This is often an age of intense cliquishness, and students who aren't part of the dominant social group can feel socially isolated in a small school.

THINGS TO CONSIDER WHEN LOOKING AT SECONDARY SCHOOLS.

- Consider what size high school would be best for your child. Many students thrive in large high schools. They love the stimulation of broad course offerings, a diverse study body and a full menu of extra-curricular activities. Such students usually find their niche through special interests: sports, school government, music or drama. However, public school educators are beginning to realize what has long been clear to small independent school educators: many students get lost in large comprehensive high schools. They cut classes and fail to do assignments because they are convinced no one cares and they have no sense of connection to the teachers, administrators, or most of the students. To give students the opportunity to feel part of a community and to feel they are important, many school districts across the nation are establishing "schools within a school" and when possible small, self-contained public high schools. In this area, a few districts are following this trend; if such an option isn't available to you, and your child seems to be one who won't find a niche in a large high school, you might want to consider a small private school.

• Ask to see representative class syllabi, textbooks, and reading lists to determine whether the school's academic requirements are appropriate to your child's needs and abilities.

If your eighth grader struggles through Jack London short stories, you probably should have second thoughts about sending him or her to a school that assigns Conrad and Hawthorne to all its ninth graders.

• Look for a school that offers extracurricular activities that will appeal to your child.

Teenagers actively involved in extracurricular activities are more likely to be happy and stay out of trouble than those who merely go to classes and come home. Look not only for a school that offers programs in your child's special interest areas but also for one that encourages and allows broad participation in extracurricular activities so that he or she can develop new interests. (The segment on "Bruce Cohn" in *Four Families* at the end of this section illustrates why extracurricular involvement can be so important to a high school student's success and happiness.)

• Ask about the school's college counseling and career guidance program.

Many public high schools have been forced to make drastic cutbacks in their counseling programs. If you choose a high school that offers little or no counseling, consider using a private counselor to help your child make college or vocational decisions. (Avoid those who make extravagant promises about their ability to get their clients into the *best colleges.*) Private high schools should provide thorough and personalized college counseling — check to see that they do.

• If you want your child to continue schooling after high school, ask to see the list of colleges and universities attended by recent graduates, and ask what percentage of students meet the minimum qualifications for acceptance to the University of California.

When students are surrounded by peers who are serious about preparing for college, they are more likely to take high school seriously. However, do not select a school because you think it is a feeder school to certain colleges (see page 34 for more on this topic.) Parents should also realize that many students attend two year colleges, not because they aren't qualified to go to a four year school but because family finances necessitate the bargain education community colleges provide. If a public high school serves a low socio-economic level and thus has a relatively small percentage of students going on to four year colleges, find out if it has a strong honors program for its motivated students.

Two other indicators of the strength of a high school's academic program are the pass rate of students enrolled at the University of California on the Subject A Exam (see appendix) and its students' performance on Advanced Placement Tests. Grades of 3, 4, or 5 on these tests qualify for credit at most of the nation's colleges. The California Department of Education (916-657-2277) releases figures on the percentage of each public high school's senior class who take these exams and how well the students perform.

• Ask about the school's policy towards ability grouping.

For years, educators have debated the pros and cons of ability grouping, sometimes referred to as tracking. Currently, many influential educational researchers argue that all students should be exposed to the kind of challenging, stimulating curriculum typical of honors classes. Many school districts are moving in the direction of heterogeneous grouping in an attempt to give all students a rigorous, academic experience. However, some teachers and parents are concerned that the move away from ability grouping will end up resulting in a watering down of the curriculum and the loss of the stimulation normally associated with honors classes. Some schools have maintained their honors program but made them less exclusive by allowing any student willing to do the extra work to take the classes.

If you have a high achieving child and a school mandates heterogeneous grouping in most or all subjects, try to ascertain whether instructors successfully challenge all their students. If you have a student who doesn't shine academically and a school does track, find out if the school adequately stimulates its average and struggling students or whether these students get stuck with un-inspiring instructors who expect little of their students.

ASK WHETHER THE SCHOOL IS ACCREDITED. Accreditation certifies to other educational institutions and to the general public that a school meets established criteria and standards and has been evaluated by an official review board. Private schools that receive public funds to educate handicapped children must be certified as meeting certain standards by the California Department of Education, but California does not accredit private schools. If a school claims it is "accredited by the State" inquire further. Legally, private schools are merely required to register with their county office of education. This simple registration procedure is in no way a form of accreditation, but some schools try to make parents believe it is.

The Western Association of Schools and Colleges (WASC) is one of six regional agencies in this country authorized by the Department of Education to accredit public and private schools. Accreditation by this private agency is especially important for secondary schools because students from unaccredited schools may have difficulty getting into some colleges. To obtain WASC accreditation, a school must complete a thorough self-study, which is followed by a three-and-a-half day visit by a team of educators. The visitation committee evaluates the school on the basis of whether the school is accomplishing its stated objectives. Once full accreditation is granted, a review occurs at least every six years. If you are considering an accredited school, feel free to ask to read the accreditation report. A school is under no obligation to show it to you, but a refusal to do so should cause you some concern. WASC reports include a section commending the school for what the school does well and a section recommending what areas the school should work at improving. If the areas of recommendation are not merely trivial and address some concerns you have, ask the school what it is doing to implement the recommendations.

While virtually all public comprehensive high schools have WASC accreditation, public elementary and junior highs rarely apply as they are already subject to a high degree of accountability under state guidelines and controls. However, because there is virtually no state control over private schools, a growing number of private elementary and middle schools are applying for WASC accreditation. The accreditation process helps them evaluate and improve their programs while also assuring the public that the school meets established standards and provides a program that successfully implements its goals and philosophy.

Accreditation is not a guarantee of excellence, and a lack of accreditation does not imply an inferior program. Accreditation is a time-consuming and expensive process, and thus many good private elementary schools, especially new ones operating on a tight budget, do not choose to apply for it.

Other accreditation or certifying organizations mentioned in this book include:

The California Association of Independent Schools (CAIS) was established in 1939 to promote high academic and professional standards for its member schools. Secondary schools seeking CAIS membership must be accredited by WASC. All member schools are required to undergo a thorough self-evaluation every six years, followed by a visit from an evaluation committee. To be considered for membership in CAIS, a school must be in operation for at least six years; after two years of operation, a school may apply for provisional membership.

The Western Catholic Education Association (WCEA) has an evaluation procedure very similar to that used by WASC. The Oakland Diocese, which oversees the operation of Alameda and Contra Costa County Catholic parish schools, has chosen to certify its schools jointly with WASC. All parish school have been accredited by WASC, but some are in the process of renewing that accreditation.

The Association of Christian Schools International (ACSI) offers to its members an accreditation program similar to the WASC instrument. Many area ACSI schools are choosing to seek dual accreditation from both organizations.

Several other religious and education organizations accredit their member schools. In most cases, the accreditation process involves a self-study and a visit by outside educators.

ANSWERS TO FREQUENTLY
ASKED QUESTIONS

When should I start investigating schools?

Although you can't start talking to friends, neighbors, and pre-school teachers too soon about school choices, the fall term before your child enters school is usually the best time to start visiting schools and evaluating your public and private school choices. If you decide in October that you do not want what your public school district has to offer, you will have plenty of time to visit and apply to other districts or private schools. Few private schools, at least in this area, are interested in taking applications more than a year in advance. While an early start will maximize your options, don't despair if you start later. For every school with long waiting lists, many more have openings up until — and even after — the school year starts.

There are two important exceptions to this schedule. Private schools with preschool programs usually give priority to children coming from their pre-kindergarten program and therefore may not have many spaces left for children applying the winter or spring before kindergarten starts. Many parents have found that to ensure their children entry into these schools, they have to enroll them in the school's preschool program. If you live in a school district that offers alternative or magnet schools, phone the district office to find out when you should apply.

What should I do if a school recommends that my child wait a year before starting kindergarten?

A child must be five years old on or before December 2 to enter a California public school kindergarten. Many private schools use a similar cut-off date, but a few will allow younger children to enter their kindergartens if they feel the child is mature enough to handle the class work. A growing number of private schools require that entering kindergartners be five by September. Most schools give a kindergarten readiness test to determine a child's level of developmental maturity. On the basis of that test, the school may recommend that a child wait a year before entering kindergarten or that the child go into a transitional kindergarten, a pre-kindergarten program offered by many private schools and public school districts. These programs typically have a smaller student to teacher ratio than the regular kindergarten classes and take into account the shorter attention span and less developed motor skills of their students.

It has become very common, especially in affluent areas where parents can afford an extra year of preschool and where schools pride themselves on running "academic" kindergartens, to start children with fall birthdays a year later even if the child appears to be developmentally ready for kindergarten. This is especially common with boys because they tend to develop fine motor skills later than girls do and because parents often are apprehensive about their son being the smallest or youngest boy in the class.

Children who are developmentally, emotionally, or socially immature should be given an extra year to mature before starting school. If there is any doubt about your child's readiness, wait a year. Later, it will be far less painful to skip a child who is too advanced for his grade than it will be to have him repeat a grade.

Should I have my child tested before I start shopping for schools?

In most cases, testing is not necessary. However, if a child appears to have learning disabilities or seems *exceptionally* bright, testing might help you determine what kind of school will best serve your child's needs. Your pediatrician, the Family Service Association, or an educational counselor should be able to refer you to a reliable professional. In some cases public school districts will test children free of charge, even before the child is enrolled in school.

How important is it that reading be taught in kindergarten?

To a certain extent, this is one of those swinging pendulum issues. Many educators in both public and private schools do not believe formal reading instruction should begin until first grade because they feel kindergarten should be a year for developing social skills, building self-confidence, and working on reading readiness. These educators point to studies that show a significant catch-up factor in reading ability — i.e., in studies of children with similar intelligence, those who aren't taught to read until first or second grade (or even later) catch up and often surpass in enthusiasm and ability those who were taught formal reading in kindergarten.

However, in the late 1970s and early 1980s, as the public reacted against the experimentalism of the previous decade, many parents demanded more structure and pressured the schools to include reading as part of the kindergarten curriculum. In response to that pressure, many public school districts and private schools began formal reading instruction in their kindergartens. Now, the pendulum seems to be swinging back as educators and parents are looking at these academic kindergartens and wondering if we're not pushing our children too hard.

Experienced kindergarten teachers realize that some of their students are ready to read and others aren't. A good program doesn't hold back those who are eager and ready to read, but doesn't pressure those who aren't. If you are considering a kindergarten that promises to teach all its students to read, be sure your child is developmentally ready for the tasks expected. Too much pressure on children early in their school careers can cause frustration and insecurity that might result in negativity towards school in general.

Can a child who starts out in public school change to a good private school later?

In most cases, yes. All private schools experience some natural attrition. Because of family moves, changes in family finances, or transfers to other schools, even the most competitive schools have occasional openings in the upper grades. And many private schools increase their class sizes in the upper grades, creating other openings. Therefore, a child who has done well in public school has an excellent chance of transferring to a private school.

Even parents with a child who has not done well in public school (a reason many parents consider making the switch) can find private schools willing to try to turn the child around. Some private schools are especially effective at taking under-achievers or "diamonds in the rough" and turning them into successes. However, some schools that take students with low test scores or grades make summer school attendance or the repetition of a grade a condition of acceptance.

Many parents are happy with public school for their children's elementary school education but wish to change them to private schools for their middle and high school years. In most cases, secular private high schools accept students on the basis of test scores, grades, interviews, and recommendations. To most admissions people, a good student is welcome and past schooling is of relatively minor importance. The most competitive (i.e., most applicants for number of places) independent schools in the East Bay all report that close to one half or more of their entering students come from public elementary schools.

Admittance to area Catholic high schools can be more difficult for the child who has attended a public elementary school since Catholic high schools give priority to graduates of feeder parish schools. However, these schools also accept large numbers of public school products.

Should I forget about sending my child to a private school if the tuition is more than I can afford?

While some small private schools cannot afford to give scholarships, many of the large and well-established schools do. Parochial schools, where fees are relatively low anyway, usually give sibling discounts, and some try to set up a certain percentage of their budgets for scholarships for parishioners. Independent schools, which tend to charge the highest tuition, are usually quite generous in granting financial aid. According to recent National Association of Independent Schools (NAIS) figures, 17% of the students at member schools receive some financial aid. Proprietary schools and new schools struggling to make ends meet tend to give few scholarships.

To what extent should I involve my child in the school selection process?

With children just starting elementary school, this is usually not much of an issue. Five- or six-year-olds are generally pretty amenable to whatever their parents think is best. However, once you've done your research it might be useful to involve your child in the final decision if you are torn between two or more schools, especially if the schools you are considering allow or require prospective students to visit for a day or two. Such a visit can allow you to consider your child's reaction to the teachers, the other students, and the playground environment.

Allowing older children to be involved in the school choice decision is much more important but also can be more complicated. Adolescents are more likely to try to do well in school if they feel that their desires have been considered. Again, if you are comfortable with several schools, then allowing your child to spend a day at each one and make the final decision is generally a good idea. However, if, for example, you believe your fourteen year old needs the structure and small classes of a private high school, but she wants to go to the public high school with all her friends, you may want to strike a bargain. Explain why you think a private school would be best and ask her to try it for a year. Chances are that once she makes new friends and sees the advantages of small classes, she will want to stay. If she doesn't, then maybe the public high school will be a better place for her. (See the story of the Stark family in Four Families.)

Are the best teachers in public or private schools?

Good teachers can be found in all kinds of schools — public and private, traditional and open. Public schools have more difficulty getting rid of weak teachers than do private schools, but private schools also have their share of "lemons." Because of public school pay increments for additional coursework and district in-service requirements, public school teachers are more likely to attend professional workshops than are their private school counterparts.

Ideally, a school should balance the experience and wisdom of older teachers with the energy and enthusiasm of younger ones. In the early eighties, public school hiring of new teachers had been virtually non-existent for almost a decade, so few had that healthy balance. Now as most area districts are experiencing increasing enrollment at all grade levels and mass retirement among their veteran teachers, they are hiring many new teachers. Some of those are former private school teachers attracted by the more attractive pay and benefits that public schools can offer.

Often, especially at the secondary level, it is easier to be a good teacher at a private school than a public one. Because class sizes are usually smaller, teachers can assign more written work and respond more thoroughly. Private school teachers don't have to put up with as many discipline problems or as much red-tape as do their public school counterparts. And private school teachers can expect more support from parents; when parents are paying a hefty sum for tuition, they're more likely to make sure their children complete their assignments and attend classes. Because of these advantages, many excellent teachers remain at private schools despite the lower pay.

Why are the "best" public schools — the ones that score the highest on the statewide tests — always in areas most people can't afford to buy a house?

High-priced neighborhoods have a concentration of well-educated professionals, and there's an obvious correlation between the academic achievement and values of the parents and their children's ability to do well in school and on standardized tests. Furthermore, these areas have few rental units, and therefore teachers don't have a large turn-over rate of students during the school year. Another explanation for the expensive housing/high test score correlation is that when children of affluent parents do struggle academically, their parents have the financial resources to send them to specialized private schools or pay for extensive tutoring.

Well-educated parents usually have high expectations for their children and feel comfortable helping their children with homework. Another aspect of the high-priced neighborhood that helps improve the schools is the availability of energetic, capable volunteers (many of whom were once teachers themselves)— parents who have the luxury of not working full-time and can serve as classroom, music, art, and library aides. These parents also have the time to be active members of their P.T.A.s. Furthermore, many affluent districts have set up foundations to raise money for the local schools and use the donated funds for such "extras" as library books, computers, and science aides and equipment.

Should I believe people when they tell me that a certain school or district is good or bad?

Unfortunately when people talk about "good" and "bad" schools, they usually are referring to the population a school serves and not the quality of the teachers, principals, and programs. Certainly, the "good" schools described above offer many advantages because they are working with children who may be easier to teach and are blessed with parents who support the schools in countless ways. However, many schools that look bad when judged by standardized test scores are excellent if they are judged by the caliber of their programs and staff. An administrator in one local district described in glowing terms the best school in his district: a school full of committed, imaginative, dynamic teachers led by a wonderful principal; however, he admitted that few people would describe this school as the best or choose to send their children there because it serves the poorest, most transient segment of the district. On the other hand, he told me that the school that is considered the district's best, i.e., has the highest test scores, is actually one of the worst—has the most burned out teachers and uninspired leadership. Before ruling out what everyone says is a bad school or district, you would be wise to investigate for yourself in what way a specific school is good or bad.

How much do test scores and other statistics tell me about how good or bad a school is?

Since schools tend to teach to the student norm, those which consistently score in the 90th percentiles are apt to have a more accelerated and demanding program than do those with much lower scores. However, parents should not choose a school purely on the basis of high scores. In many cases, high test scores tell more about the socioeconomic make-up of a school than the quality of teaching. Schools with high test scores do not necessarily have superior teachers and programs; and many schools with relatively low test scores have skilled teachers and challenging programs.

Parents should also realize that fluctuations in test scores do not necessarily mean a decline or improvement in the caliber of teaching. All schools experience years when they are blessed with especially gifted classes and years with students of more average abilities.

Schools that serve a low socio-economic population operate under clear disadvantages. Parents are less likely to have the time or background to help children with homework or serve as classroom aides, and teachers may have to spend much of their time giving extra attention to students who don't speak English. On the other hand, having a child in a high-testing school district can be a mixed blessing. While these schools are apt to be filled with many gifted students and offer a challenging curriculum, children of average intelligence or those with learning disabilities often have difficulty keeping up with their peers and thus can suffer from poor academic self-esteem.

What kind of school will be best for my very bright child?

Many area public and private schools have excellent programs for bright students. If you have a child who is extraordinarily bright, look for either a specialized school for the gifted or one that has flexible and imaginative teachers who can keep your child intellectually stimulated while encouraging social interaction with peers. Also look for schools that encourage students to participate in science fairs and other activities—e.g., the Odyssey of the Mind Program at the elementary level, the Academic Decathlon and Model U.N. at the secondary level—that allow the intellectually curious to extend their love for learning outside the classroom. Avoid placing an exceptionally bright child in a highly structured school which emphasizes group instruction and focuses primarily on basic skills.

Who should consider a boarding school?

Sending children to boarding school for their high school education is less common in California than it is on the East Coast. However, parents might consider boarding school if:

- family problems interfere with a child's academic and emotional well-being;
- a child needs a change of environment to get a second chance academically;
- they cannot find an acceptable school in their own community;
- a child seems to need the close interpersonal relationships and total school environment offered by good boarding schools.

If you are considering a boarding school, you can save yourself time, money, and disappointment by using the services of an educational counselor — an expert who specializes in matching students with appropriate schools. Avoid counselors who charge schools a commission for each student they place.

What school will give my child the best chance of getting into a prestigious college like Stanford or Harvard?

Admissions people from the most competitive private colleges assert that students with good grades, high test scores, and impressive talents and extracurricular activities will have a good chance of acceptance no matter what high school the student attends. Some area high schools, public and private, consistently have a high percentage of students accepted at prestigious colleges. However, these students are generally accepted because of their abilities and achievements, not because of any special influence their schools have.

Private high schools and public schools which serve wealthy communities also have a higher proportion of their top seniors applying to (and therefore being accepted by) expensive private colleges than do schools serving families of more moderate means. After all, if parents are already spending $10,000 or more on private school tuition or live in $700,000+ homes, they are more likely to be able to afford the $25,000+ price tag of universities like Stanford or Yale.

Parents should select high schools on the basis of philosophy, course offerings, quality of teaching, and the ability of the school to meet the student's needs. Parents who place their child in an academically competitive high school may find that because the competition is stiffer and the courses are more demanding, the child's grades are lower than they would be in a school with a more average spectrum of students. Consequently, selecting a high school with a good track record in college admissions can backfire if the school is chosen primarily because parents think it will be a stepping stone to a prestigious college.

FOUR FAMILIES

The following experiences of four Bay Area families illustrate important aspects of the school selection process. The names of the families and schools involved have been changed.

Sally Adams becomes livid when anyone mentions Greer, a prestigious school in her affluent suburban community. Sally's daughter Anne attended Greer her first three years of school, and Sally is convinced that the experience was damaging to her child's emotional and academic development.

Sally is embarrassed to admit that she selected Greer without visiting other private or public schools. "My father was willing to pay for the best education for his granddaughter, and although I had grown up here and gone to the public schools, I had heard that they were now terrible. I didn't look at other private schools because Greer was close, had been there a long time, and looked so impressive."

In the first grade, Anne began to have real problems. "She was nervous and acting out in school. She had hours of homework, and the work was just too hard. When I tried to talk to the principal or teachers, they dismissed her problems as stemming from laziness "

Sally is most angry at Greer because she feels that it was dishonest about Anne's progress. "The school inflates grades and misrepresents test scores so parents will be happy and keep their kids in the school. Despite all her problems, Anne's grades were always good at Greer. When I finally took Anne out because of her anxiety and unhappiness, Greer had me convinced that she would be way ahead of most of the public school kids. I thought her third grade year at public school would be a real breeze."

Sally had a real shock when she discovered that Anne was, in fact, way behind most of her public school classmates. "Anne didn't know the number facts, didn't understand basic math concepts, and her reading and phonics skills were weak. When the public school gave achievement tests, Anne's scores were dismal compared to those of the other children in her class. Greer had shown parents only the grade equivalences and had us believe that only its students scored above grade level. I discovered that almost all Anne's public school classmates score substantially above grade level. Unlike the public schools, Greer doesn't show parents percentages, which are the best indicators of where a child stands."

Sally admits that her daughter's problems didn't miraculously disappear once she changed schools. "Because she has some serious gaps in her basic skills, she still needs a private tutor. But we are both much happier. Anne's teacher is very supportive and understands that Anne has learning disabilities. That is something Greer never cared to recognize because it won't make allowances for individual difficulties, and, besides, most of its teachers aren't trained to recognize learning problems. Anne is now happier socially because there isn't just one tight little clique of girls like there was at Greer. After a year and a half at the public school, Anne's anxiety, which was so acute at Greer, is almost gone. Naturally, because Anne is happier, my husband and I are happier."

Sally, who is on numerous parent committees and serves as a volunteer aide, also enjoys feeling like an important part of the school community. "At Greer, we were expected to drop the kids off, pick them up, and not ask too many questions. I like knowing more about Anne's day, and I feel our relationship is more complete because I'm involved in her education."

Despite her experience at Greer, Sally does not condemn all private schools. She merely recognizes that she didn't spend enough time evaluating Greer's program and philosophy and realizes that many public schools are better than their reputations. Sally may send Anne to a private junior high and high school. But she knows that her approach will be far different the second time around. "I would look for one appropriate to my child's needs and one which has open channels of communication with parents. That may be hard to find, but it's well worth the effort."

Jim and Pat Stark learned six years ago the importance of matching a child with the appropriate school. Their older son Dave decided when he was in the eighth grade that he wanted to attend St. Mark's, a boys' prep school known for its strict discipline, rigorous academic demands, and competitive sports program. Although his family is not Catholic and had always been public school oriented, Dave chose to go to St. Mark's because he wanted the academic challenge and because several of his public school friends were also going.

Dave worked hard and did well, so when his brother Phil, two years younger, completed junior high, he too decided to leave the public school system and enter St. Mark's. Reflecting back on that decision, Phil states, "I wanted to succeed and be admired. My brother was successful there, and so I figured I would be too. My parents left the decision to me, but I knew they were pleased when I decided to follow Dave."

Jim and Pat acknowledge that the two boys had always been different. "Dave was much more self-motivated academically and things came easily to him. Phil was more social and athletic. He was always more interested in girls than his brother was, but he was also more sensitive."

Despite these differences, the Starks assumed that St. Mark's would offer Phil the same positive experience it had given Dave. However, several months into Phil's freshman year, the family began to realize that Phil was having a difficult time. Pat recalls, "He was so anxious to please us. He studied with intense diligence, but with a joylessness that gave us the feeling he was doing it for us rather than himself. That year he had a terrific amount of work and just seemed overwhelmed." Despite the effort he expended, Phil's grades the first semester hovered in the low C range, a real shock since he had always earned A's and B's in public school.

As Phil struggled with his studies, his family witnessed a troubling personality change. "Phil had always been a real charmer, very open and easy to be with. But he began to lose his self-confidence. He became very quiet and withdrawn. He would stay hunched over his desk for hours, until we called him for dinner. As soon as he finished eating, he would go right back up to study."

Phil and his parents now realize that academic pressure was not the sole cause of his unhappiness. While Dave's best friends had joined him at St. Mark's, Phil's had remained at Pierce, the public school across the street from his house. However, his inability to participate in St. Mark's highly competitive athletic program was probably the most demoralizing aspect of Phil's freshman year. "I loved basketball, but I didn't make the team. That was tough for me. I really needed that outlet. By the spring my grades had improved, and I knew I could make it through academically. I was proud of that, but, overall, I had a bad feeling about myself and school. I knew St. Mark's was teaching me good study habits, and the teachers were dedicated and caring, but all that didn't make up for what was missing for me."

The summer after his ninth grade year, Phil saw a family counselor who specializes in working with troubled adolescents. Phil's parents feel those visits helped him make the decision to return to public school. His mother recalls, "Once he made that decision, he could relax again."

Both parents note, somewhat sadly, that Phil never worked very hard at Pierce and maintained a B average with minimum effort. Despite their realization that Phil wasn't being academically challenged in the public school, Pat stresses, "I felt much better about the whole Phil. He played basketball, had girlfriends, and was much easier to get along with." Jim adds, "He had more time to hunt and spend time at our ranch, activities he'd always loved but had little time for that year at St. Mark's."

Phil, now a hard-working sophomore at a state university, knows that college might be easier for him had he stayed at St. Mark's. But he also believes that public school offered him broader educational experiences that were not available at a private school. "Because Pierce's student body was predominantly minority, I was exposed to other cultures and backgrounds. St. Mark's was just too narrow for me. I wasn't comfortable with academics taking over my whole life. When I tried to go that route, I just moved inside myself and was a pretty miserable human being."

Like the Starks, Mimi Cohn also has two very different children. Her older child Jenny has always been a bright, self-motivated student, and school choice for her was never a problem. "Adams, our public high school, was perfect for her. She was in all the honors classes, had fabulous teachers, and received an excellent education. Even if we were very wealthy, I never would have considered a private school because I can't imagine her getting a better education anywhere else."

Jenny's younger brother Bruce is also bright and was placed in the gifted program in junior high school. "But," notes Mimi with a sigh, "he was a gifted child who didn't want to work. His teachers, recognizing his laziness, did not recommend him for the honors classes at Adams." Bruce's grades were good his first year of high school, but his parents were displeased with how little effort he expended. "The school just doesn't challenge the kids much if they're not in the honors group. However, Bruce seemed happy enough that first year so we accepted his lack of academic motivation with resignation."

At the end of Bruce's freshman year, the Cohn's school district closed one of its three high schools. Mimi describes that year as traumatic for everyone. "There was a huge influx of new students and staff, and the transition was tough on everyone." Because Bruce had always been shy and overly sensitive, his mother believes he was especially affected by the confusion. "Bruce sat in the back of his very large classes and did nothing. He became less social and wasn't involved in any extra-curricular activities — even sports, which he had always loved." Bruce's parents became most concerned when they discovered he had been cutting history, and the school never let them know. "He was getting an A just by copying his friends' notes. When I contacted the school about his cutting classes, the teachers and counselors kept telling me they would do something, but they never did."

By the end of his sophomore year, Bruce's parents realized their son needed a different school. "At home we were having constant battles, and the tensions created by Bruce's problems affected us all." The private day schools in the area were either full or didn't seem right for Bruce. At that point, Bruce told his parents he was willing to try a boarding school, and so Mimi contacted an educational consultant. After interviewing the Cohns and Bruce, the consultant recommended three schools that still had openings and would serve Bruce's needs. In retrospect, Mimi is very glad that they spent several hundred dollars to get professional advice. "I had no idea how to start looking for a good boarding school. We would have dragged Bruce around for weeks and spent far more money trying to find the right school on our own."

The Cohns selected Shannon School, a small prep school in Southern California, which, according to the consultant, did a good job at motivating underachievers. The school, impressed by Bruce's test scores, accepted him for the eleventh grade and gave him a partial scholarship. Even with financial assistance, the Cohns had to dip into savings intended for Bruce's college education. "But," Mimi says, "we realized that if he stayed in public school, he might never even make it to college."

Bruce's performance his first year at Shannon surpassed his parents' expectations. He received all A's and B's, partly his mother admits because "as a new student that first grading period, he was required to spend his evenings in a supervised study hall." But Bruce and his parents were also pleased that attending a small school allowed him to star in athletics. At Adams, he hadn't even tried out for a team, but at Shannon he made varsity soccer, basketball, and baseball. The most unexpected dividend of Bruce's boarding school experience was his involvement in the arts. Bruce had taken a little piano and trumpet when he was younger but hadn't done anything musically for years. He had a free period, so the school put him in the band. Then, on his own, he started taking piano lessons from the music teacher, who soon had him composing his own music. "Music," states his mother, obviously pleased, "has now become an important part of his life. He still composes music to relax. What's even more remarkable," continues Mimi, "is that Bruce was in a play his senior year. That would never have happened at Adams."

Mimi feels one of Shannon's greatest strengths was its college counseling. "If Bruce had still been at home, I would have gone mad trying to get him through his applications. The public school counselors just have too many students to give much individual aid. Shannon's counselor not only made sure the students completed their applications correctly and promptly but also did a good job recommending appropriate colleges. Knowing Bruce's past, the school steered him towards small schools where he would have a chance to shine."

Mimi acknowledges that her son did have some difficulties during his two years at Shannon. "Despite his success that first year, he almost didn't return for his senior year because he missed the freedom and social life of home. But he went back because he wanted to go to a good college and knew returning to public high school would be a real risk." During that second year, some of Bruce's old habits re-appeared. "When he had a teacher he didn't like, he just refused to work, and his grades dropped. However, the staff helped him pull through, and he was accepted to all the colleges he applied to."

In trying to assess why Shannon was so good for Bruce, Mimi attributes much of its success to size. "Because he had an opportunity to succeed in several activities, his self-esteem naturally improved. And with small classes, students couldn't get away with cutting or slacking off without the teachers knowing." Mimi doesn't think Shannon's teachers are necessarily better than those at Adams, although they tend to be younger and more energetic. "Small classes allow the faculty to be more effective with kids like Bruce. It's easier to be a better teacher with only 15 students, instead of 30 or 35, in a class. The public school teachers have so many students that they, quite understandably, focus on the ones like my daughter who want to learn " Mimi also believes that boarding school was good for Bruce because it allowed him to get away from his achieving sister. "It was healthy for all of us to be off his back. When he came home for vacations, we were all more relaxed, and he and Jenny began to get along for the first time in years."

Mimi is still grateful that the public high school gave her daughter such an excellent education. But she knows that Bruce's experience there was not unique. "Our public school serves two levels well — the top and the bottom. But not enough is done for the average or unmotivated kids. I'm not sure what the answer is, but I'm afraid a lot of them fall through the cracks as Bruce was doing."

When Nick and Jan Ryan went house hunting, their first priority was to find a house within walking distance of a neighborhood public school. Nick explains,

"Education has always had a high priority in our family. We had heard from friends that the public schools were a mess, but we really wanted our children to receive a public education." Jan adds, "I didn't plan to work until the children were older, and I was willing to work very hard to help improve the schools." Despite their determination, the Ryans' experience with Grant, their "friendly little neighborhood school," turned out to be a nightmare.

The Ryans believe Grant's biggest problem was its principal. "He was politically ambitious — eager to move on to a more powerful position in the district office. Consequently, he was never around and rarely considered the children's interests when he made decisions." The Ryans were also dismayed by the incompetency of the kindergarten and first grade teachers. Jan recalls with a sigh, "The kindergarten teacher was obsessively neat. She was most comfortable when the kids huddled quietly in the corner watching Captain Kangaroo. When children became too noisy, she taped their mouths shut. She didn't like equipment with a lot of pieces which might mess up the room. And when she did art projects, she wanted the finished products to be all the same."

The Ryan children remember the first grade teacher as being even worse. Sam, the younger son, relates, "We were terrified of her. She really seemed to hate kids."

Despite her dissatisfaction with the principal's indifference and the teachers' unprofessionalism, Jan remained determined to help improve the school. Her husband recounts his wife's efforts. "Jan put all her energy into that school. She became the P.T.A. president and organized a parent volunteer program. She even took a class at her own expense so she could start a motor fitness program for the children, something the staff had no interest in doing themselves."

All that determination to stick with Grant dissolved in the Ryans' third year at the school. Sam, now in the seventh grade, recalls the incident that drove the family to surrender. "I was in the first grade. The class troublemaker was acting out again, so the teacher phoned the mother to come get the child. The woman arrived with a belt, and in front of the whole class the teacher let the mother whip the kid. We were supposed to close our eyes, but we could hear him screaming. The teacher told us not to tell our parents about what had happened, but some of us did." Within several weeks, the Ryans, along with two other families, had found a new school for their children.

The Ryans decided to take advantage of their district's open enrollment policy, and they were also determined to use their painful lessons from Grant to set up criteria for what they were looking for in a school. "We wanted a dedicated, harmonious faculty and an active parents' group. But most of all, we wanted a warm, involved principal who was tending the ship." After several weeks of talking to friends and visiting schools, the Ryans enrolled their children in Brodie, a racially mixed school in another middle class neighborhood.

The entire Ryan family is convinced that Brodie's principal, Mr. Peters, is responsible for making his school as good as Grant was bad. Nick succinctly summarizes Mr. Peters' kindness and dedication with the comment, "That man walks on water." The children describe in more detail the wonderful Mr. Peters. "Sometimes he substitutes; he tutors kids having difficulties; he is always on the playground at lunch." Jan is most impressed by "this man's ability to stand up for his faculty while also keeping the kids' interests his top priority. He knows how to work with his staff and help them become better teachers."

According to the Ryans, Mr. Peters' concern and warmth permeate the entire school, creating a true feeling of community. "The school's parent group is active and enthusiastic, constantly raising money and bringing special programs to the school. The teachers spend free periods and lunch hours offering help sessions, and they constantly take classes to improve their teaching skills." Jan acknowledges, "Certainly not every teacher there is fabulous, but there is the expectation that everyone will be good, so even the average teacher rises to those standards. At Grant the feeling had been that a good teacher threatened the others by making them look bad."

Once Mark, the Ryan's older child, reached the sixth grade, the family found itself facing another dilemma — where to send the children for junior and senior high school. Although the district claimed that all its schools were equally good, the Ryans knew that their assigned junior high was very weak academically. Jan, who tutors university students lacking basic skills, did not want to take the chance that her own children would need similar help when they entered college.

Many of the children at Brodie go on to what Nick describes as "a very good public junior high school, but that option was not available to us because the school already had its quota of Caucasian families." Nick adds, "perhaps we could have clawed our way into that good junior high; we knew a few families who did that. But we were reluctant to go through the uncertainties of that process. We didn't want to be bouncing the children around from school to school. Besides, at the time that school was changing principals, and there were a lot of politics going on in the district office. We didn't want to go through another Grant experience."

During Mark's last year at Brodie, the Ryans very methodically compared their private and public school options. The family made a list of what they wanted in a school. "First of all, we wanted a well-balanced school, a place that would offer the children lots of opportunities in the arts, sports, and academics. We also wanted a school that did a thorough job of teaching writing skills and had strong science and history programs." After six months of visiting schools and talking to parents, the Ryans enrolled Mark in Duff, a well-established K-12 independent school.

Nick states that leaving the public school system caused them a lot of anguish. "But Duff could serve our children's needs and our expectations as parents. Our public school choices just couldn't do that." The Ryans, now in their third year at Duff, cite many factors that convince them that they made the right decision. Many of these factors stem from the class size (16-20 students) and the relative smallness of the school. Jan believes that small classes have been especially important to Sam. "He is shy, and in a large class he could get away with never participating. But at Duff no one is anonymous, and the kids participate in everything." Sam adds, "In a public school I never would have made the team, but at Duff I'm on the J.V. basketball team. I'm not very good, but the better players help me out." Both Mark and Sam also like the feeling of knowing almost everyone in the school and participating in activities with students of all grade levels.

The Ryans are also delighted that Duff's teachers are not tenured. "Most of the teachers are excellent, but it's reassuring to know that when incompetent ones do turn up, they aren't around very long." The Ryans' list of Duff's advantages is lengthy and includes excellent college counseling, school trips, caring staff, and the wide participation of students in all aspects of school life. But all agree that they most value Duff's atmosphere of trust. Nick explains, "The public schools, understandably, must run on rules and regulations. At Duff a love of learning and respect for each individual pervades the whole school. The children rarely abuse that trust."

The Ryan children also point out some not-so-obvious advantages. Mark believes that "at Duff, it's easier to be yourself. The pressure to conform, to be and dress like everyone else, was stronger at Brodie." Sam sees less racism among the students. "Our public schools had a lot of minority students, but there wasn't much real mixing. The racial groups remained pretty separate. At Duff, race isn't important in determining who your friends will be."

The Ryans have changed their feeling about the role of private education. Jan states, "When the kids were young, we saw private schools as elitist institutions and an unnecessary expense. Now, although I have had to go back to work to pay for the tuition, we are very grateful for Duff's existence." Nick adds, "We still support public schools and hope that they get the financial and moral support that they need to solve some of their problems. At Brodie, we saw how good a public school can be, but we've also seen how important private schools are in serving children's needs when the public schools can't do that."

DIRECTORY OF PUBLIC SCHOOL DISTRICTS

Piedmont Avenue School, Oakland, 1926
Courtesy of Charlotte Walker Gill

EXPLANATORY NOTES FOR PUBLIC SCHOOL LISTINGS

If you do not know what school district you reside in, telephone your County Office of Education listed at the beginning of each county's district listings. School districts are listed alphabetically by county and your district of residence can tell you your child's assigned school.

In the spring of 1995, every school district in Alameda and Contra Costa counties was asked to complete a questionnaire for this book. Some districts filled out these questionnaires completely and took advantage of the opportunity to share with the public a description of the programs offered in their schools. Others provided only basic information.

Class and school size: Because of enrollment changes and contract agreements with teacher unions, average and maximum class sizes may vary year-to-year. Many public schools use paid and volunteer instructional aides, thus making the adult-to-student ratio lower than the stated class size indicates. The average class size in junior and senior high schools varies greatly from course to course; academic classes usually have fewer students than do physical education and typing. In many districts, a maximum class size is set as part of the contract agreement with teachers. In instances where a class exceeds the stated maximum, the district must get approval from the teacher or hire an extra classroom aide. Districts were also asked to state the average enrollment of their schools.

On site day care is noted as **EDC**. Districts were asked to indicate which of their schools have on-site day care and whether these programs are available to parents during school holidays. On site day care is offered by a variety of providers: non-profit agencies such as the YMCA and city recreation departments, and proprietary day care centers. Some districts indicated which providers serve their schools, but most did not. Principals often have a list of licensed day care homes and local daycare centers that serve children attending their schools.

Transportation: During the years of budget cuts, bus service was one of the first items slashed in most districts. A few districts, especially those in which students live great distances from school campuses or in which children must

47

take dangerous routes to school, have retained transportation services. All districts must by law provide transportation for disabled students.

Alternative programs: Districts were asked to explain alternative programs (see page 8) in some detail. Some high school districts did not describe programs such as independent study or work study because they do not operate as alternative schools. All unified and high school districts have continuation schools (see page 9.)

Transitional Kindergartens (Trans Kdg.): Districts were asked to indicate if they offer a program for children who are legally old enough to attend kindergarten but who are not developmentally ready.

GATE: As is explained on page 11, programs for students designated as gifted or talented vary greatly from district to district. School districts were asked to indicate how their schools serve their GATE students.

Open/Closed Campuses: Many of today's high school campuses are open — i.e., students are free to come and go during lunch and their free periods. Other districts, in response to parental and community concern, have maintained or reinstated closed campuses and thus forbid students to leave campus during the school day without permission. Some districts have a modified form of the open campus — e.g., students may leave campus only during lunch or only if they are seniors.

Couns:student ratio: High schools were asked if they have a counseling staff serving their student body and to indicate the ratio of counselors to students.

High School districts were also asked the percentage of graduates attending four year and two year colleges, and the percentage of students participating in extracurricular activities. Some districts did not have this information available.

Bonds and Parcel Taxes: Using information compiled by EDSource of Menlo Park, I have listed which districts have passed school bond and parcel tax elections since 1987.

DISTRICT BOUNDARIES
ALAMEDA COUNTY

ELEMENTARY, HIGH SCHOOL &
UNIFIED SCHOOL DISTRICTS

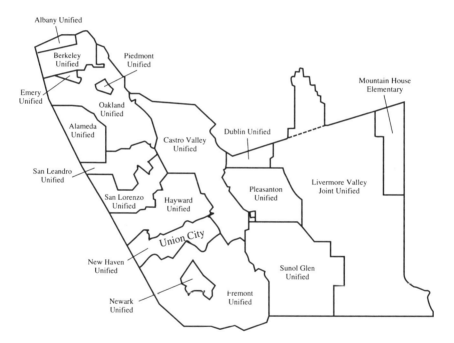

ALAMEDA COUNTY PUBLIC SCHOOL DISTRICTS

Alameda County Office of Education
313 West Winton Ave.
Hayward, CA 94544-1198
(510) 887-0152

ALAMEDA UNIFIED SCHOOL DISTRICT. 200 Central Ave., Alameda 94501. (510) 337-7070. Dennis Chaconas, Superintendent. 10,055 students. Elem. schools: Eight K-gr. 5, three K-gr. 7 year-round (Bayfarm, Paden, & Washington) ; avg. enrollment 450; avg. class size 27, max. 28, aides used K-gr. 5. Three gr. 6-8 mid. schools; enrollment 700-820; avg. & max. class size 28. Trans. Kdg. Three elem. sites offer EDC. Business & military partnerships, two roving elem. teachers, music teachers in mid schools, computer labs in all schools. Pullout GATE program. Two high schools: avg. enrollment 1100, 6 period day, Spanish & French, 2 music teachers. Summer programs at elem. & secondary schools. 1989 bond raised $47.6 mil. for site acquisition and improvement.

ALBANY UNIFIED SCHOOL DISTRICT. 904 Talbot Ave., Albany 94706. (510) 559-6500. J. Dale Hudson, Superintendent. 2,902 students. Two K-gr. 2 elem. schools, avg. enrollment 162; two K gr. 5 clem schools, avg. enrollment 508. (Note: between 1998-2000 district will have 3 elem. schools with enrollment of 400-500.) Avg. & max. class size 28; instructional aides in all elem. schools & all grades, also used in ESL & spec. ed. classes. EDC: 7:30 am-6 pm at MacGregor; from 3-6 pm at Cornell & Marin. Computer lab at Cornell. Science, instrumental & vocal music for gr. 4-5. 4 wk. summer program for K-gr. 12, enrichment main focus.

Albany Mid. School gr. 6-8; 684 students; avg. class size 30, max 31. Instrumental music, Spanish & French, counseling, special day class, computer lab, art classes, wood shop, extensive noon intramurals, afterschool sports for boys & girls.

Albany High, 870 students. Open campus. One couns.: 375 students. Avg. class size 28, max. 30. 7 period day. French & Spanish; 5 AP classes.

Heterogeneous grouping in all social studies & Eng. classes in gr. 9-10. Competitive science program (natl. champions); Mathletes; small group counseling; R.O.P video program; special day class; aggressive college placement program; high participation in athletic program; substance abuse prevention/rehabilitation; programs to address underprivileged minorities, low income, 1st generation to attend college; fin. aid & college nights for parents; freshman parents support group; adult school volunteers tutor students. 63% of students participate in extra-curricular programs. 52% of grads. go to 4 yr. colleges; 47% to 2 yr.

1993 bond raised $31 mil. for a new mid. school to open in fall of '97 (est.). Current mid. school will become elem. site. Between 1996-2000, Albany H.S. will undergo extensive new building, re-building & renovation. In 1987 and 1990 parcel tax passed to maintain programs.

BERKELEY UNIFIED SCHOOL DISTRICT. 2134 Martin Luther King Jr. Way, Berkeley 94704. (510) 644-6257. Jack McLaughlin, Superintendent. 7,965 students.

1995-96 is a transition year as the district begins to implement its restructuring plan. By the '96-97 school year, there will be ten, K-gr. 5 elem. schools (300-450 students/school) and three gr. 6-8 middle schools (600 students/school). Parents may request any elem. school within their attendance zone. While all elem. schools teach the same general curriculum, each one will have its own focus. Some emphasize technology, while others offer a rich arts curriculum; one has a farm in the middle of the campus. Students are assigned to one of two middle schools depending on their attendance zone or can apply to the Longfellow School of Performing Arts and Technology. For a complete description of each school's program and instructions regarding enrollment procedures, parents should obtain "Guide to Berkeley Schools" from the superintendent's office.

Avg. class size in K-gr. 5, 25; max. 29; aides in all grades. Avg. mid. school class size, 27, max. 30. Bussing to elem. schools within attendance zones and for students w/ special needs. EDC at all elem. sites from 7:30 am-5:30 pm; open on school holidays. Instrumental music, libraries, computer labs. GATE pull-out 1/2 day/wk. Summer programs. Parcel tax passed in 1986, 1990, and 1994. '94 tax, to last for 12 yrs., will be used to reduce class size, support enrichment programs, and pay for instructional materials. 1992 bond raised $158 mil. to rebuild or refurbish all schools. Parcel tax passed in '86, '90 & '94 for reduction of class size, enrichment, and instr. materials. District foundation raises $100,000 +/yr.

Berkeley High School. 2400 students. Avg. class size 28. Campus closed except at lunch. Latin, German, French, Spanish, Swahili. 12 AP courses. Selected seniors take course at UCB through Accelerated High School Program. African-American Studies Dept. Tutoring widely available. The Finance,

Biotechnology, Media and Computer Academies combine course work with summer jobs, internships & mentoring programs. 75 clubs and activities include Mock Trial, Midnight Soccer, NOW, & Environmental Club. Jazz Ensemble, newspaper, yearbook, & literary mag. have received natl. recognition. Extensive renovation of entire campus in process. 75% of student body participates in extracurricular activities. 1 couns.: 400 students. 70% of grads. attend 4 yr. colleges, 15% attend 2 yr.

East Campus Continuation School. Alternative high school program for students who need extra academic assistance in a smaller school with small classes. Individualized instruction, self-paced program. Students referred through high school counselors or by parental request.

CASTRO VALLEY UNIFIED SCHOOL DISTRICT. P.O. Box 2146, Castro Valley 94546. (510) 537-3000. FAX: (510) 886-7529. Robert J. Fisher, Superintendent. 6,771 students. Eight K-gr. 5 elem. schools; one gr. 6-8 mid. school, one comp. high school, one alternative high school.

DUBLIN UNIFIED SCHOOL DISTRICT. 7471 Larkdale Ave., Dublin 94568. (510) 828-2551. Dr. Vince Anaclerio, Superintendent. 3,506 students. Three K-gr. 5 elem. schools, avg. enrollment 600, avg. class size 29, max. 32. One gr. 6-8 mid. school, 770 students, avg. class size 28-30, max. 37 (band & PE). EDC offered by private providers at all elem. sites. Business partnerships, instrumental music (gr. 4-12), computer labs. Extended day GATE program. Summer enrichment for gr. 1-8, skills for gr. 7-12. New District Foundation raises about $20,000/yr. 1993 bond raised $36 mil. for school renovation and energy conservation.

Dublin High School: 800 students, two counselors. Avg. class size 27, max. 37 (band & PE). Open campus, 6 period day. Career Center, 5 AP classes, French & Spanish

EMERY UNIFIED SCHOOL DISTRICT. 4727 San Pablo Ave., Emeryville 94608. (510) 655-6936. FAX: (510) 655-3339. J.L. Handy, Superintendent. 583 students. One K-gr. 5 elem. school; one gr. 6-8 mid. school; one gr. 9-12 high school.

FREMONT UNIFIED SCHOOL DISTRICT. 4210 Technology Dr., Fremont. (510) 657-2350. FAX: (510) 770-9851. Sharon Jones, Superintendent. 28,928 students. Twenty-eight K-gr. 6 elem. schools; avg. enrollment 546; avg. class size 28, max. 30. Five gr. 7-8 jr. highs; avg. enrollment 882; avg. class size 29, max. 30. Aides used in Special Ed. & bilingual classes. 14 elem. sites offer private child care programs, 8 offer Y.M.C.A. Latchkey Programs. Trans. Kdg. Bussing avail. for some students. Computer labs at most schools. Inst. music at Jr. High. Business partnerships with over 100 companies & organizations. GATE program at all schools; some pullout, some cluster. Award-winning Bilingual Programs in Spanish &

Mandarin. District Independent Study Program at Vista School for K-gr. 12; Opportunity School for gr. 7-9. District Foundation raises about $22,000/yr. 1991 bond raised $81 mil. for school construction and improvement.

Five comprehensive high schools: avg. enrollment 1480; avg. class size 28, max. 30. Six period day. Instrumental music, tutorial services. French, Spanish at all sites; German at one site; Mandarin at one site. 40 AP classes and prep. classes offered at the 5 sites.. 35% students participate in extracurricular activities. 39% of grads. attend 4 yr. colleges, 43% 2 yr. colleges. Continuation high school.

HAYWARD UNIFIED SCHOOL DISTRICT. P.O. Box 5000, Hayward 94540. (510) 784-2600. FAX: (510) 782-7213. Marlin Foxworth, Superintendent. 20,115 students. Twenty K-gr. 6 elem. schools, two K-3 schools, one gr. 4-6 school. East Ave., Bowman, Eldridge & Park operate year-round. Five gr. 7-8 int. schools. Three comp. high schools, one alternative high school. English Language Center.

LIVERMORE VALLEY JOINT UNIFIED SCHOOL DISTRICT. 685 E. Jack London Blvd., Livermore 94550. (510) 606-3200. Dr. Joyce C. Mahdesian, Superintendent. 11,024 students. Eleven K-gr. 5 elem. schools, avg. enrollment 500-600, avg. class size 30, max. 32. Four gr. 6-8 mid. schools, avg. enrollment 725, avg. class size 30, max. 32. All elem. sites have extended day care 7 am-6 pm, but space limited; open on school holidays. Computer labs and time-out rooms at all sites. Instrumental music gr. 4 & 5, strings/orchestra. GATE at all sites, programs vary. Summer programs. District foundation.

Two comprehensive high schools, avg. class size 25-30, max. 30-35. 6-8 period day. Spanish, French, German. 7 AP courses, 21 honors classes. Career centers, business partnerships, computer labs. 28-30% of students attend 4 yr. colleges; 50-55% attend 2 yr. Two continuation high schools, one alternative high school.

MOUNTAIN HOUSE ELEMENTARY SCHOOL DISTRICT. 3950 Mountain House Rd., Byron 94514. (209) 835-2283. FAX: 835-0284. K-gr. 8 school, serves 27 students at intersection of Alameda, Contra Costa, and San Joaquin counties. One classroom of K-gr. 3, one class of gr. 4-8. Avg. class size 15, max. 20. Instructional aide helps in both classrooms. Computer lab: K-gr. 3 learn keyboarding; gr. 4-8 students spend at least 30 min./day at computer. Transportation provided by district's school bus that can also take entire school on field trips & overnight excursions. Older students attend week of science camp. Teachers experts at individualizing instruction & collaborative learning for multi-age classroom. Trans. Kdg. Will accept out-of-district students if space avail. EDC: 6 am-6 pm, open on school holidays if needed. Most students go on to Tracy Union High.

NEW HAVEN SCHOOL DISTRICT. 34200 Alvarado Niles Rd., Union City 94587. (510) 471-1100. FAX: (510) 471-7108. 12,941 students. Six K-gr. 4 elem. schools, avg. enrollment 800 students, avg. class size 30, aides used in all grades. Trans. Kdg. EDC at all elem sites from 7 am-6 pm, closed on school holidays. Three gr. 5-8 mid. schools, avg. enrollment 1200 students, avg. class size 30. Fine Arts instruction, Healthy Start, computer labs, business partnerships, collaboration with upper level schools and colleges. GATE: cluster grouping in language arts, math and fine arts. Summer programs at school sites: summer school, sports camps, city recreation & YMCA programs.

One comp. high school; 3800 students; avg. class size 30, max. 33. Closed campus. 7 period day. One couns.: 500 students. 9 AP classes. French, Spanish, Tagalog, German, Russian, & American Sign Language. Business partnerships, college readiness programs, tutoring program, early academic outreach, Otis Spunkmeyer college readiness program, SIP & Chapter 1, Migrant Education, African-American Mentoring, Second Chance counseling services. All seniors required to complete 20 hrs. of community service. 25% of grads. attend 4 yr. colleges, 40% attend 2 yr. One alternative high school.

1993 bond raised $55 mil. for school renovation & technology. District Foundation sponsors the New Haven Olympics, summer sports camps, K-gr. 12 tutoring program, a college scholarship program and an annual Fine Arts performance. Within 3 yrs. all schools will be interconnected through a fiber network to bring technology into the classroom.

NEWARK UNIFIED SCHOOL DISTRICT. P.O. Box 385, 5717 Musick Ave., Newark 94560. (510) 794-2141. FAX: (510) 794-2199. Gerald K. Trout, Superintendent. 7,192 students. Eight K-gr. 6 elem. schools, avg. enrollment 480, avg. class size 30, max. 32. One gr. 7-8 mid. school, 950 students, avg. class size 30, max. 32. Open enrollment. Six. elem. sites offer EDC from 7 am-6 pm; open on school holidays. All elem. schools have Reading Recovery Program and California Early Literacy Learning for primary classes. Resource, science & P.E. teachers at all schools. Bilingual and sheltered English classes. Computer labs and computerized library collections. All schools have business partnerships. Before and after school instrumental music instruction. GATE: integrated in classroom and afterschool program for gr. 4-6. Opportunity class for mid. school students. Home schooling program for K-gr. 12. District foundation raises $130,000+/yr. 1990 bond raised $12 mil. for library, classrooms, & pool.

One comprehensive high school: 1800 students, avg. class size 30, max. 35. Closed campus for gr. 9, open for gr. 10-12. One Couns.: 900 students. Avg. class size 30, max. 35. Six period day. Spanish, French, & German. Six AP classes. Mock Trial & Academic Decathalon. Peer tutoring programs & math tutoring center. Academic Core Enrichment Program. Library fully automated with internet accessibility. Art gallery, 360 seat theater, photo lab w/ digital image, state-of-the-art computers w/ laser discs. 36 athletic teams, 22 clubs, drama & leadership program. Puente Program helps Mexican American/Latino students succeed in school and continue on to college by enlisting mentors from the community and involving parents in their children's education. Bridgepoint continuation program located on campus. School Resource Officer on campus to ensure safety and to facilitate communication between the school community and the Newark Police Dept.

OAKLAND UNIFIED SCHOOL DISTRICT. 1025 Second Ave., Oakland 94606. (510) 836-8100. Carolyn Getridge, Superintendent. 51,748 students. 59 elem. schools, grade range varies but most are K-gr.6, twelve operate year-round. Six mid. schools for gr. 5, 6, or 7 through gr. 8; nine jr. highs for gr. 7-9. (The district is planning to restucture all or most of its schools in a more uniform configuration: K-gr. 5, gr. 6-8, and gr. 9-12). School and class size vary. Most schools have business partnerships and varying amounts of computer technology. Instrumental music at some sites. Tutoring programs throughout the district. Some schools serve specific neighborhoods, others are magnet schools open to students from throughout the district. 1994 bond raised $170 mil. for school safety programs.

Three gr. 9-12 & three gr. 10-12 high schools, enrollment ranges from 400-1200. Open campuses. 6-8 period day. Tutorial programs. One couns.: 325 students. Most schools have several business partners. 35% of grads. go to 4 yr. colleges, 50% to 2 yr. Each high school offers one or more academies, speciality programs which provide students with academic instruction, career development, and assigned mentors.

Elem. & Jr. High Magnet Programs: Art School, K-gr. 8; Cole Performing & Visual Arts, gr. 4-8; Emerson Science, K-gr. 5; Grass Valley Science & Technology, Academy for Young Scientists & Authors, K-gr. 6; Kaiser Arts & Humanities, K-gr. 8; Lazear Science & Technology, Eng-Spanish Bilingual, K-gr. 1; Parker Environmental Science & Technology, K-gr. 6; Claremont Computer & Technology, gr. 7-8; King Estates Environmental Science & Natrl. Resources, gr. 7-9.

High School Magnet Academies: Castlemont: Computer Technology, International Trade & Transportation, Envir. Science & Natrl. Resources; Fremont: Media & Mass Communications, Architectural Design & Construction; McClymonds: Business & Interntl. Finance, Law & Govt.; Oakland: Visual Arts; Oakland Tech.: Pre-Engineering, Health & Bioscience; Skyline: Performing Arts, Future Teachers.

For information regarding magnet programs and enrollment procedures phone Student Services (836-8111) or Magnet Programs (836-8614).

PIEDMONT UNIFIED SCHOOL DISTRICT. 760 Magnolia Ave., Piedmont 94611. (510) 420-3600. Gail G. Anderson, Superintendent. 2,454 students. Three K-gr. 5 elem. schools, enrollment ranges from 323-539 students, avg. & max. class size 28, aides in all grades. Trans. Kdg. All elem. sites have EDC run by Piedmont Rec. Dept., $3.25/hr. Piedmont Mid. School: gr. 6-8, 657 students, avg. & max. class size 28. Music program at all levels. Theatre Arts, Dance. GATE Program being restructured; UCB Academic Talent Development Program for 8th graders.

Piedmont High School: 680 students, avg. class size 24, max. 30. 7 period day. Spanish, French, German, Mandarin. 11 AP courses. Theatre, musicals, debate, dance. Accelerated High School Students Program at UCB. College and Career Center; one couns.: 272 students. 80% of grads. attend 4 yr. colleges, 16% attend 2 yr. 90% of students participate in extracurricular activities. **Piedmont Independent Learning High School**, 40 students, offers basic education, personal counseling, and career guidance in an alternative program. Individualized instruction, work experience opportunities, flexible scheduling, small classes.

Piedmont Educational Foundation, active parent group at each school. Parcel taxes passed in '85, '89 and '93 to maintain & improve ed. programs. 1994 bonds raised $24 mil. to renovate schools and athletic field.

PLEASANTON UNIFIED SCHOOL DISTRICT. 4665 Bernal Ave., Pleasanton 94566. (510) 462-5500. Bill J. James, Superintendent. 9,707 students. Seven K-gr. 5 elem. school, avg. enrollment 675, avg. class size 32, max. 32-33. Two gr. 6-8 mid. schools, avg. enrollment 1117, avg. class size 34. All elem sites have day care from 7 am-6 pm; some remain open on school vacations. English Language Development, GATE, afterschool study program, computer education, vocal and instrumental music. Pleasanton Partnerships in Education Foundation Programs: mini-grants for teachers for classroom projects; Excellence in Education award program for teachers; drug awareness program; adopt-a-class program. 1988 bond raised $85 mil. to improve facilities. Summer programs at elem. & secondary schools.

"Discovery" Program at Walnut Grove Elem.: alternative program that combines individualized and personalized instruction with learning centers and hands-on learning. Three classrooms (K/1, 2/3, 4/5) so students have same teacher for two years. Integrated curriculum emphasizes critical thinking, concrete understanding and cooperative learning techniques. Parents expected to work in the classroom, at home or through the workplace to support the program. Open to all students in the district but priority given to students in Walnut Grove attendance area and to siblings of students in the program.

Two comprehensive high schools, avg. enrollment 1300 students. One couns.: 499 students. Six period day. 38% of grads. attend 4 yr. colleges, 53% attend 2 yr. colleges. English language development, GATE, R.O.P. Support services include health clerks, psychologists, speech & language specialists, career centers, peer help program. AP classes.

SAN LEANDRO UNIFIED SCHOOL DISTRICT. 14735 Juniper St., San Leandro 94579. (510) 667-3500. FAX: (510) 667-3569. Thomas Himmelberg, Superintendent. 6,712 students. Seven K-gr. 5 elem. schools (Garfield operates year-round); two gr. 6-8 mid. schools; two high schools.

SAN LORENZO UNIFIED SCHOOL DISTRICT. 15510 Usher St., P.O. Box 37, San Lorenzo 94580. (510) 481-4600. FAX: (510) 278-4344. Janis A. Duran, Superintendent. 9,438 students. Nine K-gr. 7 elem. schools, avg. enrollment 680 students, avg. class size 29, max. 33. Six sites offer EDC, 7 am-6 pm. Business Partnerships, computer labs, G.A.T.E., music, Reading Recovery. Healthy Start Grants at 4 sites. Multi-age Primary Program at Lorenzo Manor. Summer programs.

Two gr. 8-12 comprehensive high schools: avg. enrollment 1600 students, max. class size 33. Six period day. Computer lab, music, French, Spanish, German, 7 AP classes. Business Partnerships, Safeway Academy, Career Paths, Block Scheduling. One continuation school.

SUNOL GLEN. P.O. Box 569, Main & Bond Sts., Sunol 94586. (510) 862-2026. FAX: (510) 862-0127. Diane E. Everett, Superintendent. 206 students. One K-gr. 8 school. Avg. class size 23, max. 25. Transportation. EDC: 6 am-6 pm, open on school holidays. Music program, computer & science lab. Interdistrict transfers accepted. Most graduates attend Foothill High School in Pleasanton.

DISTRICT BOUNDARIES
CONTRA COSTA COUNTY

ELEMENTARY, HIGH SCHOOL &
UNIFIED SCHOOL DISTRICTS

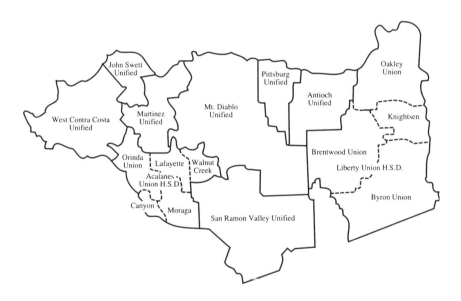

CONTRA COSTA COUNTY PUBLIC SCHOOL DISTRICTS

Contra Costa County Office of Education
77 Santa Barbara Rd.
Pleasant Hill, CA 94523
(510) 942-3388

ACALANES UNION HIGH SCHOOL DISTRICT. 1212 Pleasant Hill Rd., Lafayette, CA 94526. (510) 935-2800. FAX: (510) 932-2336. Dr. James Pereino, Superintendent. 4233 students. District serves students from Lafayette, Moraga, Walnut Creek, Canyon & Orinda school districts. Four comp. high schools, enrollment ranges from 907-1186 students. Closed campuses. Avg. class size 26, max. 31. Seven period day. Spanish, French, German. 9 AP classes. 80% of students participate in extracurricular activities. Business partnerships, ROP classes, tutorial centers, LEP services, peer counseling. One couns.: 405 students. 1988 bond raised $34 mil. to acquire & improve school sites. 1991, 10 yr. parcel tax used to maintain programs; 1995 parcel tax used to ensure continuation of 7 period day, maintain small classes, improve libraries and add technology. District foundation raises about $75,000/yr.

ANTIOCH UNIFIED SCHOOL DISTRICT. 510 G. St., Antioch 94509. (510) 706-4100. FAX: (510) 757-2937. Alan Newell, Superintendent. 14,904 students. All elem. & jr. highs operate year-round. Ten K-gr. 6 elem. schools, avg. enrollment 886 students. Max. class size: K, 33; gr. 1-3, 32; gr. 4-6, 31. EDC offered at Sutter, Muir, Kimball, London from 6:30 am-6 pm, open on school vacations. Two gr. 7-9 jr. highs, avg. enrollment 1600, max. class size 31. (Once third mid. school and new high school open, elem. schools will be K-gr. 5, mid. schools will be gr. 6-8, high school gr. 9-12.) Computer labs, instrumental music instruction in all schools. Strong business partnerships. District has made large financial commitment to technology. Strong teacher in-service, active P.T.A's. Extensive special education classes & programs, including preschool program. Young Authors; competitive speech, spelling bee and science fair participation. Exemplary science center to refurbish and deliver elem. science kits. GATE: gr. 3-5, pull-out program one day/wk.; mid.

61

school, meets one period daily; h.s., AP classes. Intersession classes for elem. & mid. school students. District Foundation raises about $75,000/yr.

One gr. 10-12 comp. high school: 2300 students. (Starting with the '96-'97 school year, the district will have two high schools and will offer two career-path academies, in multimedia & marketing.) 7 period day. Spanish, French, 7 AP classes. Students self-select into honors and AP classes. 40% of students involved in extracurricular activities. 63% of grads to to 4 yr. colleges, 20% to 2 yr. colleges; One continuation high school. Prospects—Independent Study for gr. 7-12, 466 students.

BRENTWOOD UNION SCHOOL DISTRICT. 250 First St., Brentwood 94513. (510) 634-1168; FAX: (510) 634-8583. 2,667 students. Three K-gr. 4 elem. schools, avg. enrollment 450, avg. class size 27, max. 30. Aides used in all grades. One gr. 5-6 school, one gr. 7-8 school, 570 students in each, avg. & max. class size 30. EDC at Ron Nunn & Garin, 6 am-6 pm. All schools run year-round. Transportation offered on fee basis. Music & art specialist for K-gr. 4, instrumental music for gr. 5-8, Write to Read Labs for K-1st, Josten's Labs gr. 2-3, computer labs at all schools, counselors at all schools. GATE: K-gr. 6, pull-out enrichment; gr. 7-8, honors classes. Summer school. 1990 bond raised $9.8 mil. to construct & improve facilities. District feeds into Liberty H.S. District.

BYRON UNION SCHOOL DISTRICT. 14401 Bryon Hwy., Bryon 94514. (510) 634-6644. FAX: (510) 634-9421. Margaret Green, Superintendent. 890 students. One K-gr. 5 elem. school, classroom aides. One gr. 6-8 mid.school. Avg. class size 25, max. 30. Transportation. EDC through YMCA at Discovery School 6 am-6 pm. Computer labs & music instruction. Pull-out GATE program. Four wk. summer school in proficiency & enrichment. Out-of-district students accepted for child care, employment or personal reasons. District feeds into Liberty H.S. District.

CANYON SCHOOL DISTRICT. P.O. Box 187, Pinehurst Rd., Canyon 94516. (510) 376-4671. FAX: (510) 376-2343. Jennifer Loshonkohl, District Coordinator. One K-gr. 8 school, 65 students, avg. class size 20, max. 25. Out-of-district students accepted if space in class. Entire school has art, Orff music & eurythm on Fridays. Two computers in each classroom. Creek, redwood grove on school grounds. GATE program imbedded in classroom curriculum. Multi-age grouping, problem solving, TRIBES type activities. Summer art program.

JOHN SWETT UNIFIED SCHOOL DISTRICT. 341 B St., Crockett 94525. (510) 787-2355. FAX: (510) 787-2049. Jon Frank, Superintendent. 2,087 students. District serves students in Rodeo and Crockett. One K-gr 5 elem. school, 1070 students, avg. & max. class size 31, aides used in all grades, EDC 3 hrs./day. One gr. 6-8 mid. school, 650 students, avg. & max. class size 31. Bussing avail. One comp. high school, 590 students. One cont. high school,

20 students. Computer instruction, spec. ed. programs in all schools. High school has band & voc./tech. classes. Summer programs for gr. 6-12.

KNIGHTSEN SCHOOL DISTRICT. P.O. Box 265, 1923 Delta Rd., Knightsen 94548. (510) 625-0073. FAX: (510) 625-8766. Vicki Rinehart, Superintendent. One K-gr. 8, year-round school, 325 students. Avg. class size 28; max. 30 (K-gr. 3) 32, (gr. 4-8). Aides 1 hr./day in each grade. Transportation. Computer lab; instrumental music, gr. 4-8; classroom music, K-gr. 5. Swimming pool used for P.E. in fall and spring. GATE program offered through elective program 4 days./wk. Modified traditional calendar: students start early Aug.; 2 wk. break in Oct., Dec., & March; 6 wk. break June-July. District feeds into Liberty H.S. District.

LAFAYETTE SCHOOL DISTRICT. P.O. Box 1029, 3477 School St., Lafayette 94549. (510) 284-7011. 3140 students. Four K-gr. 5 elem. schools, enrollment 380-775 students. One gr. 6-8 mid. school, 1044 students. 1992, 8 yr. parcel tax used to maintain & improve educational programs. District feeds into Acalanes H.S. District.

LIBERTY UNION HIGH SCHOOL DISTRICT. 20 Oak St., Brentwood 94513-1195. Daniel Smith, Superintendent. (510) 634-2166. FAX: (510) 634-1687. District serves 2370 students living in Brentwood, Bryon, Knightsen, & Oakley School Districts. One comprehensive high school, 2040 students; one continuation school, 120 students, one alternative high school, 210 students. All schools operate year round. District passed $10 mil. bond in 1988 to improve facilities; 1994 bond raised $25 mil. to construct new school.

MARTINEZ UNIFIED SCHOOL DISTRICT. 921 Susana St., Martinez 94553. (510) 313-0480. FAX: (510) 313-0476. Dr. Scott Brown, Superintendent. 3872 students. Four K-gr. 5 elem. schools; avg. enrollment 450; One gr. 6-8 jr. high, 900 students. Avg. class size in all schools 28, max. 30; aides used in gr. 1-3. All elem. sites offer EDC, 7 am-6 pm,; open on school vacations. 3 also have preschool day-care. All sites participate in Martinez Ed. Foundation Busikids program, partnering businesses with classrooms, departments & sites. All have instrumental music and networked computer centers that are on the Internet. Vocal music in K-gr. 5. GATE: In K-gr. 5, cluster grouping within the schools as well as 2 hr. pull out once a wk. Home School Program for parents teaching children at home under the direction of MUSD. Opportunity Program for gr. 6-8 students at risk who need smaller class size. 5 wk. remedial & enrichment summer program for gr. 1-8. District foundation raises about $50,000/yr. 1988 bond raised $25 million to improve facilities. 1995 bond raised $23 mil. to renovate jr. high and improve other sites.

Alhambra High School: 1000 students. Closed campus. One couns.: 450 students. 7 period day. 15% of grads. attend 4 yr. college, 25% attend 2 yr. 79% of students participate in extracurricular activities. Spanish, French, 4 AP classes. School wide writing center equipped with computers plus 2 other computer centers, wide area network to other schools and internet; state-of-the-art library media center. Vicente Martinez H.S.: offers small group instruction & support for at risk students, same grad. reqrmnts. as Alhambra H.S.

MORAGA SCHOOL DISTRICT. P.O. Box 158, 1540 School St., Moraga 94566. (510) 376-5943. FAX: (510) 376-8132. 1788 students. Two K-gr. 5 elem. schools, avg. enrollment 590 students. One gr. 6-8 mid. school, 615 students. 1992, 8 yr. parcel tax used to maintain & improve ed. programs. District feeds into Acalanes H.S. District.

MT. DIABLO UNIFIED SCHOOL DISTRICT. 1936 Carlotta Dr., Concord 94519. (510) 682-8000. FAX: (510) 680-2505. Robert Baum, Superintendent. District serves 34,064 students from Bay Point, Clayton, Concord, Pleasant Hill and parts of Martinez & Walnut Creek. Twenty-eight K-gr. 5 elem schools, avg. enrollment 590, avg. class size 30, max. 34; aides used in all grades. Nine gr. 6-8 mid schools, avg. enrollment 875, avg. class size 30, max. 37. Most elem. sites offer EDC. Business partnerships, instrumental & vocal music, computer labs. Pull-out GATE program. Independent Study Program for K-gr. 12 at Horizons School. Summer school programs for all grades.

Six comprehensive high schools, avg. enrollment 1470. Spanish, German, French. Radio station, Technology Academy, Health Services Academy Six "necessary small high schools" for at-risk students who need a smaller, more nurturing school environment, enrollment 33-60 students.

OAKLEY UNION ELEMENTARY SCHOOL DISTRICT. P.O. Box 7, 91 Mercedes Lane, Oakley 94561-0007. (510) 625-0700. FAX: 625-1863. Frank J. Hengel, Superintendent. 4000 students. Four K-gr. 5 elem. schools, avg. enrollment 700, avg. class size 28.5; aides used in all grades. One gr. 6-8 mid. school, 1,150 students, avg. class size 23. Open enrollment. No out of district students being accepted. EDC at Gehringer, Laurel, & Vintage Parkway. Laurel & Vintage Pkwy. are year-round (YRE) schools, closed only three wks. in July. Three other schools on a "modified traditional calendar"—begin in early Aug. with 2 wk. breaks in Oct., December, & March. Instrumental music & computer labs in all schools. Special programs at various schools include Homework Club, Peer Tutoring, Reading Chair, Academic Olympics, 6th gr. Science Camp. Awesome Authors Program won Golden Bell Award. Pull-out GATE program. Summer programs. Intersession programs for YRE students. District feeds into Liberty H.S. District.

ORINDA UNION SCHOOL DISTRICT. 8 Altarinda Rd., Orinda 94563. (510) 254-4901. FAX: (510) 253-0719. Richard Winefield, Superintendent. 2271 students. Three K-gr. 5 elem. schools, avg. enrollment 520. One gr. 6-8 int. school, 705 students. 1994, 5 yr. parcel tax used for maintenance, books & materials. 1995 bond raised $16 mil. to renovate existing schools. District feeds into Acalanes H.S. District.

PITTSBURG UNIFIED SCHOOL DISTRICT. 2000 Railroad Ave., Pittsburg 94565. (510) 473-4321. Robert Newell, Superintendent. 9,043 students. Seven K-gr. 5 elem. schools (one year-round), avg. enrollment 575, avg. class size 30, max. 34. Trans. Kdg. Two gr. 6-8 mid. schools, avg. enrollment 1000, avg. class size 32, max. 36. Choral music gr. 1-12, instrumental music gr. 6-12, art docents, K-gr. 6. GATE: cluster & pull-out. Opportunity programs for gr. 6-8 in a self-contained program for at least 60% of the day. Pittsburg High School: 1850 students, 7 period day, closed campus, honors & AP classes. Independent Study Center & Continuation H.S. Summer programs at 4 sites.

SAN RAMON VALLEY UNIFIED SCHOOL DISTRICT. 699 Old Orchard Dr., Danville 94526-1058. (510) 837-1511. FAX: (510) 837-9247. Biefke Vos, Superintendent. 17,788 students. Nine K-gr. 5 elem schools, 365-668 students; six K-gr. 6 elem. schools, 452-640 students; three gr. 6-8 mid. schools, 646-1085 students; one gr. 7-8 int. school, 892 students. Three comprehensive high schools, 1600-1830 students. District serves students from Alamo, Danville, & San Ramon. 1991 bond raised $40 mil. to construct, renovate facilities.

WALNUT CREEK SCHOOL DISTRICT. 960 Ygnacio Valley Rd., Walnut Creek 94596. (510) 944-6850. Michael De Sa, Superintendent. 3067 students. Five K-gr. 5 elem. schools, avg. school size 400; one gr. 6-8 mid. school, 1023 students. Avg. class size 29, max. 32. Aides in K-gr. 5, varies w/ site. Open enrollment; out-of-district accepted when space avail. EDC at all elem. sites; avail. during school holidays & summer. Business partnerships, instrumental music, jazz band, computer & science labs. Pull-out GATE program. Implementing new technology plan. New gym at mid. school. Summer programs offered in conjunction with City of Walnut Creek. 1995 bond raised $24 mil. for structural repairs. District foundation raises about $100,000/yr. District feeds into Acalanes H.S. District.

Parkmead Active Learning School (PALS), (510) 944-6858. K-gr. 5, school-within-a-school at Parkmead, offers integrated, non-competitive instruction; parents contribute 60 hrs./yr. by working in the classroom, on committees, or on at-home projects. Monthly parent meetings, close parent-teacher communication. "PALS' multi-age classroom format allows each child to learn at his or her own pace, in a supportive, stimulating environment that invites questions, exploration, and experimentation."

WEST CONTRA COSTA UNIFIED SCHOOL DISTRICT. 1108 Bissell Ave., Richmond 94801. (510) 234-3825. FAX: (510) 236-6784. Herbert Cole Jr., Superintendent. District serves 31,881 students from El Cerrito, El Sobrante, Hercules, Kensington, Pinole, Richmond, and San Pablo. 38 elem. schools (grade configurations vary), 5 middle schools, 5 senior high schools, 2 continuation high schools, 6 alternative high school sites, 2 special education centers, 9 state-funded preschools.

DIRECTORY OF
PRIVATE SCHOOLS

St. Mary's School, Oakland, 1958.
Courtesy of the Chancery of the Archdiocese of San Francisco

EXPLANATORY NOTES FOR PRIVATE SCHOOL LISTINGS

In the spring of 1995, every private school registered with the offices of education in Alameda and Contra Costa Counties and listed as having at least 12 students was sent a questionnaire. A few schools wished only to be listed in the directory and stated that parents should telephone the school office for further information. Others chose not to respond to all of the questions. No private school was deliberately excluded from the survey or omitted from this directory.

Schools are divided by county into three sections— elementary, secondary, and special education. If a school fits into more than one category, it may be cross-referenced. The elementary schools are listed by geographical groupings and then divided into three categories: Roman Catholic, other religious affiliations, and secular. Those listed in the last category include independent, proprietary, Montessori, and Carden schools.

Note: All information in the directory portion of this book was provided by the schools themselves. The author can not guarantee that the information provided is accurate. Parents should use the directory merely as a tool to ascertain what schools might meet their needs, and then evaluate the schools for themselves, using the guidelines provided in the first section of this book and their own parental instincts.

School day hours are noted as **SDH.**

Extended day care is noted as **EDC.** Most, but not all, private schools that have extended day care charge extra for this service. Schools were also asked to indicate if child care was available on school holidays. If you need extended day care but are interested in a school that doesn't offer it, ask whether local day care centers or licensed homes serve children from the school.

Class size: Average and maximum class size can vary from year to year and by grade and course offering. Many schools use aides and/or specialists in areas like physical education and music so that the student/staff ratio is smaller than the average class size, but only a few schools indicated that ratio on the questionnaire.

Tuition: Schools were asked to list their tuition and incidental fees for the 1995-96 school year, but some had not yet set the figure and so gave the '94-'95 fees. Preschool fees are not listed. Most schools raise tuition at least every two or three years; many raise it annually. Unless otherwise noted, the tuition listed is per year.

Scholarships: Schools were asked to indicate whether they grant scholarships and then asked to approximate the percentage of students receiving financial aid. Because the amount of financial aid available often varies year-to-year, many schools just indicated **fin. aid avail.** to show that tuition reductions are granted to needy students when possible. Some schools reserve scholarship money for students who are already in the school but whose families can no longer afford tuition.

Transportation: Many private schools can be reached by public transportation, and most schools help parents arrange car pools. When schools offer transportation for an extra charge, this service will be indicated in the listing.

Special programs: Schools were asked to list any special facilities and programs beyond basic academic instruction. Some did this in great detail; others did not. Therefore, some schools may have extras like computer labs and afterschool sports even though they are not listed.

Application procedures: Many schools have application deadlines, but most schools continue taking students as long as space is available. Almost all schools give priority to siblings of students currently enrolled in the school as long as the sibling is academically qualified. Schools with religious affiliations also give priority to members of the sponsoring church. To the best of the author's knowledge, no school listed in this directory discriminates on the basis of race, color, or national origin.

Accreditation: See explanation on page 27.

Secondary Schools were asked to indicate whether they have a closed or open campus (see page 48) and what percentage of their graduates attend four and two year colleges. They were also asked for their average SAT scores (see explanation in appendix) and the percentage of students who usually take the test; some schools provided this information but many did not.

Philosophy: The third paragraph of each listing includes the school's stated philosophy but does not convey the author's own evaluation of the extent to which that philosophy is carried out.

Special Education: Schools that specialize in serving students with special needs are listed in the Special Education section for each county. Most private schools will take students with learning disabilities if they feel the student can benefit from their program; schools were asked to indicate whether they have on-site learning disability (**LD**) specialists to help those students.

ALAMEDA COUNTY
PRIVATE ELEMENTARY SCHOOLS

Albany ◆ Berkeley ◆ Emeryville

CATHOLIC SCHOOLS

SCHOOL OF THE MADELEINE. 1225 Milvia St., Berkeley 94709. (510) 526-4744. Michel Calegari, Principal. Betsy Harvey, Admissions. Est. 1936. Non-profit.

K-gr. 8, 315 students. $2760-$3260; sibling discounts. 5% receive fin. aid. SDH: K, 8-1 or 10-3; gr. 1-8, 8-3. EDC: 1-6 pm, $2.75/hr, closed on school holidays. Avg. & max. class size 35; classroom aides. Uniforms. Spanish for all grades, music, computer & science lab, library. Afterschool chess club, Great Books, basketball, volleyball, track. Families contribute 20 hrs./yr. Apply by end of Feb., waiting list. July summer school for enrolled students. Accredited by WASC.

"We direct our efforts toward developing the whole child in a stimulating environment. We emphasize growth in the spiritual, psychological, intellectual, social and physical realms, recognizing the dignity and unique potential of each child."

ST. JOSEPH THE WORKER. 2125 Jefferson Ave., Berkeley 94703. (510) 845-6266. Carol Atacor, Principal. Est. 1878. Non-profit.

K-gr. 8, 155 students. $2500. Reg. fee $100. No fin. aid. SDH: 8:15-2:55. EDC: 7 am-6 pm, closed on school vacations. Avg. class size 20, max. 35. Uniforms. Band, computer enhanced instruction, family counseling service, French. Afterschool girls' & boys' basketball, softball, track & cross country, volleyball, brownies. Accessible by B.A.R.T. Apply by end of Aug. Parents contribute 30 hrs./yr. 4 wk. summer school. Accredited by WASC.

"St. Joseph the Worker School Community works together to instill a Christian spirit in its students; to prepare students to become responsible Christian members of the world community; to build upon the parents' responsibility for their children's religious and moral development; to affirm and appreciate cultural and ethnic diversity; to implement an educational program where children are taught the skills and processes necessary for critical thinking."

SECULAR SCHOOLS

THE ACADEMY. 2722 Benevenue Ave., Berkeley 94705. (510) 549-0605. FAX: (510) 549-9119. M. Ben Mohamed, Head. Est. 1969

K-gr. 8, 105 students. K-gr. 5, $5600; gr. 6-8, $5900. SDH: K-gr. 5, 8:30-3 (2:20 on Fri.); gr. 6-8, 8:30-3:10 (2:20 on Fri.). EDC: 7 am-6 pm. Dress code. Avg. class size 15; student/teacher ratio 5:1. Location of campus gives students access to local libraries, parks & other facilities. Reading, math, French & P.E. begin in kdg. All students study science, social studies, current events, art & music. Gr. 6-8 departmentalized; Latin & Humanities introduced in gr. 6. Classes supplemented by field trips relating to classroom studies. Afterschool study hall & math lab. Accredited by National Independent Private School Association.

"The Academy offers a curriculum that is both traditional and academic while providing opportunities for creative experience and expression. . . The Academy has its classroom doors open to parents who are strongly encouraged to participate in school life. . . The Academy's curriculum rests upon the premise that strong basic skills and concepts form the foundation of learning. We believe that students who master these skills early become self-disciplined and self-motivated individuals . . ."

BERKELEY MONTESSORI. 2030 Francisco St., Berkeley 94709. (510) 843-9374. Curt R. Chamberlain, Director. Est. 1963. Non-profit.

PreSchool-gr. 7 (8th grade to be added in 1996). K, $4392-$6213 (full day); 6-10 yr. olds, $5677-$7391 (full day); 11-14 yrs, $6270. Inc. fees, $270-$490. 5% sibling discount. 13% receive fin. aid. SDH: K, 8:30-1 or 8:30-3; gr. 1-7, 8:30-3 (2:00 on Fri.). EDC: 7:30 am-6 pm; $3.50/hr. for drop-in. Avg. class size (2 teachers) 22, max. 24. Specialists teach Spanish, Japanese, music, movement, art. Hands-on math, creative writing, Great Books program, computers. Campus close to park, library, UCB, BART. Middle school: community service projects, field & camping trips, week-long internships; students work in cooperative groups and learn conflict resolution. Parents contribute 20 hrs./yr. Variety of afterschool workshops and sports. Apply by mid-March; enrollment remains open until spaces full. Waiting list. Two 4 wk. summer session for preschool-9 yrs. Accredited by AMS.

BMS provides a "Montessori-based learning environment whose foundation rests on the child's natural ability and desire to learn. Its positive, stimulating environment facilitates each child's individual learning style and encourages critical thinking and problem solving skills."

BERKWOOD HEDGE. 1809 Bancroft Way, Berkeley 94707. (510) 843-5724. Est. 1976. Non-profit teacher collective.

K-gr. 6; 108 students. $5,650. Inc. fees $200. 25% receive fin. aid. SDH: 9-3. EDC: 7:30 am-6 pm; $3/hr., closed on school holidays. Avg. & max. class size 20. Large multi-purpose room, library. Specialists teach Spanish, recorders, music, PE & drama. Parents volunteer 3 hrs./mo. Afterschool chess, drama, art & cooking. Waiting list.

"Each child at Berkwood Hedge is seen as a unique, whole person, with his or her own learning style, special contributions to the community, and pattern of growth. . . we foster the children's confidence and self-esteem, encouraging children to be themselves completely, so that they become creative thinkers and expressive individuals, while being good friends and responsible community members."

BLACK PINE CIRCLE. 2027-27th St., Berkeley 94710. (510) 845-0876. Frances Kandl, Director. Est. 1971. Non-profit.

K-gr. 8, 154 students. K-gr. 5, $6350; gr. 6-8, $7560. Inc. fees K-5, $350; gr. 6-8, $450. 9% receive fin. aid. SDH: K-gr. 1, 8:45-2:30; gr. 2-5, 8:45-2:55; gr. 6-8, 8:45-3:10. EDC: 7:30 am-6 pm, closed on school holidays. Avg. class size 15-20, max. 20-22. Part-time aides in K-gr. 2 if class at max. size. Specialists teach Spanish, art, P.E., music (instrumental & singing), math enrichment. Science lab, large music & assembly room, gardens for nature study projects. Orff/Kodaly approach to music. Choral singing in all grades, recorders in gr. 4-8. String orchestras, mixed ensembles, glee club. Plays, recitations, & musical performances given by a different class each Fri. All-school picnics, games days, art fairs, music festivals; field trips to concerts, plays, museums, ballets & sites of natural & historical interest. Separate building for arts & drama; extended day center. Upper School (gr. 6-8): French, computers, science lab; all classes taught by specialists; variety of extra-curricular courses. Active parents' group. Application period Dec.-March. Child must be 5 by 12/31 for kdg.

"By steering a middle course between the skill and textbook oriented traditional institution and the more unstructured open classroom, Black Pine Circle has provided nourishment for both the intellectual and emotional development of its students. It offers a quality education in a convivial, non-competitive environment. . . The high academic level is aimed at the bright, motivated child. Emphasis is placed on reasoning skills, imagination, the 'inquiry' approach and student initiative."

THE CROWDEN SCHOOL. 2401 Le Conte, Berkeley 94709. (510) 644-2299. Anne Crowden, Director. Est. 1983. Non-profit.

Gr. 5-8; 40 students. $7500. Books & materials $500. 5% receive fin. aid. SDH: 8-3:10. Avg. class size 10, max. 12. Monthly performances, chamber music at all school functions, annual spring concert for the general public, preparation for music competitions, flexible schedule for students with outside musical commitments. English, history, French, math, science, P.E. & art. School visits & interviews Nov.-Feb. Academic & musical entrance exams in Feb. Waiting list. Afternoon extension classes include strings, creative movement, eurhythmics, recorder, youth choir. Summer program for ages 3-13 includes a variety of music & art classes and production of a children's opera.

"The purpose of the School is to provide an environment for musically gifted children....Although the School is characterized by its distinctive music program, the *primary goal* is to give the children a first-class education *in balance* with their musical needs. The highest standards will be expected from each child according to individual abilities."

EAST BAY FRENCH-AMERICAN. 1009 Heinz St., Berkeley 94710. (510) 549-3867. Marcel Barchechat, Director. Thierry Durandard, Admissions. Est. 1977. Non-profit.

PreK-gr. 6; 495 students. $7000-$8300. 14% receive fin. aid. SDH: K, 8:30-3; gr. 1-5, 8:30-3:15; gr. 6-8, 8:30-3:30. EDC: 7:30 am-6 pm; $4/hr; open on school holidays. Avg. class size 18, max. 21. Specialists teach music, art, computer, PE, drama. For the 1st 3 yrs. (PreK-gr. 1) students in immersion program with 1 hr/day of English. In gr. 2, 2 hrs. of Eng./day. Program totally bilingual in gr. 3-8: science, history, math, art & music co-ordinated in both languages. Afterschool enrichment classes. Non-French students admitted in PreK-gr. 1; French students admitted at all grades. For kdg. must be 5 by Sept. 1. 26% of students are French citizens or have dual citizenship. Summer camp for enrolled students. Accredited by C.A.I.S. & French Ministry of Education.

The school "offers a complete bilingual education at the elementary level. Curriculum is coordinated in the French and English language to instill academic skills and provide intercultural experiences. Ecole Bilingue's goal is to provide academic excellence in a multicultural environment."

EAST BAY WALDORF. 1275 61st St., Emeryville 94618. (510) 547-1842. Est. 1980. Non-profit.

K-gr. 8. $5650-$6190. 40% receive fin. aid. SDH: K, 8:30-12:30; gr. 1, 8:30-2; gr. 2-8, 8:30-3. EDC: 12:30-5:30, $3/hr., open on some school holidays. Dress code. Wooden flutes, recorder, strings, chorus, eurythemy, handwork (knitting, sewing, crochet, clothes design, claywork, drawing, painting). German, Spanish. Specialists teach orchestra, for. languages, crafts, eurythmy, sports. Parents help with all aspects of the school. Applications taken year-round. Child must be 4 yrs. by April 1 for fall kdg. Waiting list in some grades. Accredited by Association of Waldorf Schools of North America (AWSNA).

"We educate the whole child (head, heart, and hand) through consistent integration of the arts and sciences. Each individual's capacities are nurtured in the context of a community. Powers of wonder, imagination, observation, creativity, and musicianship are developed in all children. We provide an environment respectful of childhood by limiting the influence of competition, the media and fashions in the elementary grades."

GROWING LIGHT MONTESSORI. 2075 Eunice St., Berkeley 94709. (510) 527-8760. Rachel LaField, Director. Proprietary. Est. 1986.

Infant-gr. 3. Part-time $475/mo; full day $650. Inc. fees $235. 6% receive fin. aid. SDH: K, 8:30-1:30; gr. 1-3, 8:30-3. EDC: $3/hr., open during school holidays. Avg. class size 12; aides. Pottery, music, dance & body movement, swimming at public pool, visits to Lawrence Hall of Science. Year-round enrollment. Waiting list. Must be 4.5 yrs. for kdg. entrance. Summer programs.

We "teach and inspire the students with tenderness and respect. We foster a complete sense of well being working with the 'whole' child."

MONTESSORI FAMILY SCHOOL. 1850 Scenic Ave., Berkeley 94709. (510) 848-2322. Jane Wechsler, Director. Est. 1981. Non-profit.

2 yrs.-gr. 6. $5500. Inc. fees $400. 25% receive fin. aid. SDH: K, 9-3; gr. 1-6, 8:45-3. EDC: 8 am-6 pm; $3.50/hr.; open on school holidays. Avg. class size (w/ 2 teachers) 22, max. 26. Campus across from UCB and near tennis, basketball & volleyball courts, and parks. Specialists teach Spanish, science, drama, art, music, poetry & movement. On site LD specialist. Drama program culminates in a production. Parents contribute 15 hrs./yr. Afterschool basketball & drama. Apply by mid-March for elem. grades. Waiting list. Summer programs. Accredited by American Montessori Society.

"The Montessori Family School provides individual support and education for each of its unique students. The standard of academic excellence is very high in our traditional Montessori setting. Our students flourish here in many ways. We also emphasize 'teaching tolerance' and conflict resolution in the safe environment our school provides. In this way we hope to prepare our students to resolve differences in a peaceful & direct manner. The motto of our school is 'Education for Peace.'"

NEW AGE ACADEMY. 1009 Camelia St., Berkeley 94710. (510) 524-1629. Gloria Cooper, Director. (510) 524-1629. Gr. 6-8, 32 students. $6500.

"New Age Academy's Mission is to empower adolescents to make a successful transition into young adulthood by nurturing and promoting intellectual, emotional and social growth."

PACIFIC RIM INTERNATIONAL. 5521 Doyle St., Emeryville 94608. (510) 601-1500. Christina Cheung, Director. Est. 1989. Proprietary.

Preschool-gr. 6. $5450 (school day); $7160 (includes extended day care). Materials $275, school improvement fee $100. No fin. aid. SDH:8:45-3:15. EDC: 7:30 am-6 pm.; avail. on some school holidays. Avg. & max. class size 24, aides when class size is over 12. Dress code. Chinese-English & Japanese-English bilingual, multicultural education in a Montessori-based environment. Chinese brush-painting, martial arts, arts & crafts, music & creative movement, violin lessons. Montessori and bilingual specialists. Summer programs.

". . . Our aim is to furnish children with a rich and nurturing environment which caters to the development of the five senses, assist children in learning to communicate in English and Mandarin or Japanese. . .teach children an awareness of and concern for the ecological balance of nature. . . encourage children to develop self confidence and the ability to think critically and creatively. . . cultivate in children an understanding and appreciation of beliefs and practices across cultures."

SHELTON'S PRIMARY EDUCATION CENTER. 3339 Martin Luther King Jr. Way, Berkeley 94703. (510) 652-6132. Sharon McGaffie, Director. Est. 1974. Non-profit,

K-gr. 5. $4300. Inc. fees $400. No fin. aid. SDH: 9-3. EDC: 7 am-6 pm; $100/mo., free for Kdg.; closed during school holidays. Avg. class size 15, max. 20; classroom aides. Near BART & A.C. Transit. Uniforms. Library, computer center, art, music, foreign languages. Team teaching in gr. 1-5 so students taught by specialists. Active P.T.A; parents contribute minimum of 10 hrs./yr. Free hot lunch for kdg., avail. for fee for gr. 1-5. Afterschool classes in dance, drumming etc. for extra fees. Summer academic & recreational programs. Future site expansion.

"S.P.E.C. is the school with a vision for African-American children and believes that all children can enjoy and experience success in learning at their individual skill level when provided with an interesting, challenging environment and a supportive, nurturing atmosphere."

WALDEN CENTER AND SCHOOL. 2446 McKinley Ave., Berkeley 94703. (510) 841-7248. Est. 1958. Non-profit.

K-gr. 6, 94 students. $510/mo. $30-$50 trip fees. 17% receive fin. aid. SDH: K, 9-2:30; gr. 1-3, 9-3. EDC: 7:45 am-6 pm; $3.50/hr; open on school holidays. Avg. class size 16, max. 18; classroom aides. A teacher collective committed to having a diverse student body. Large art studio; drama/music studio; arts based curriculum. Specialists teach Spanish, visual arts, drama, movement & music. Parents contribute 50 hrs./yr. Summer programs vary. Call in the fall for admission for following year.

"Walden's founders believed that creative, artistic expression is an integral part of a progressive, academic curriculum. To this day, the staff supports the value of experiential learning and cooperative endeavor. The children at Walden learn an appreciation and respect for the racial, ethnic and religious diversity of their East Bay community through the school's non-sectarian and multicultural learning environment."

Alameda ◆ Oakland ◆ Piedmont

CATHOLIC SCHOOLS

CORPUS CHRISTI. One Estates Dr., Piedmont 94611. (510) 530-4056. Kathleen Murphy, Principal. Est. 1956. Non-profit.

K-gr. 8, 288 students. $262-$360/mo.; sibling discounts. Inc. fees $170. Fin. aid avail. SDH: K, 8:15-11:15 or 12-3; gr. 1-8, 8:15-3. EDC: 8 pm-6 pm.; $2.65-$3.65/hr.; closed on school holidays. Avg. & max. class size 32. Dress code. Computer & science lab, P.E., library, auditorium. Specialists teach computer, music, Spanish. Gr. 6-8 departmentalized. Emphasis on service projects. Afterschool CYO, student council, choir. Apply by April 1. Accredited by WASC.

Our goal is "to build a community and to develop the talents of each individual child, to create a warm, safe, loving environment for all to succeed."

SACRED HEART. 675 41st St., Oakland 94609. (510) 652-2220. Robert Ratto, Principal. Est. 1880. Non-profit.

K-gr. 8; 205 students. $2400; sliding scale, sibling discounts. Inc. fees $200. 75% receive fin. aid. SDH: 8-2:30. EDC: 7 am-6 pm, $2/hr. Dress code. Avg. class size 20-25, max. 30. Title II reading specialist 4 times/wk. Afterschool computers, Spanish, ballet, basketball, volleyball, track. Parents perform service hours. Accredited by WASC.

"At the heart of our teaching is our belief in the gospel message of Jesus. The gospel embraces all people and challenges us to teach and live as Jesus did. We are especially dedicated to providing quality Catholic/Christian education to the inner city of Oakland."

ST. ANTHONY. 1500 E. 15th St., Oakland 94606. (510) 534-3334. K-gr. 8.

ST. AUGUSTINE. 410 Alcatraz Ave., Oakland 94609. (510) 652-6727. Mary Ann Lemire Mattes, Principal. Est. 1918. Non-profit.

K-gr. 8; 265 students. $2800; sibling discounts. SDH: 8:10-2:55. EDC: 7 am-6 pm; $2.35/hr., closed on school holidays. Avg. & max. class size 30; aides in k-gr. 4. Uniforms. Afterschool basketball, track, cross country, softball, volleyball, cheerleading.   Single parents contribute 15 hrs./yr., couples 30 hrs./yr. or donate extra $20/hr.   Apply by April 1, testing begins in Feb. Accredited by WASC.

St. Augustine's philosophy is to "foster in students a strong, positive self-image, emphasizing the dignity and uniqueness of each individual; to foster in our students a 'world vision' not only through study but also through the exploration of social justice issues and individual moral responsibilities."

ST. BARNABAS. 1400 Sixth St., Alameda 94501. (510) 521-0595. Mr. La Russa, Principal. Est. 1958. Non-profit.

K-gr. 8; 225 students. $2200, sibling discounts. Inc. fees $230. No scholarships. SDH: K, 8-11:15 or 11:30-2:45; gr. 1-8, 8-2:45. EDC: 7 am-6 pm; $3/hr; closed on school holidays. Avg. class size 25, max. 35. Uniforms. Computer lab, P.E., music. Gr. 6-8 departmentalized. 5 day hot lunch program, meals cooked on site. Afterschool girls' & boys' volleyball & basketball for gr. 3-8.   Parents contribute 12 hrs./yr. Apply by Aug. 1. WASC accreditation in progress.

"St. Barnabas provides academic excellence and a caring, positive atmosphere. Quality education is provided by our dedicated, well-trained teachers and staff who serve as positive role models."

ST. BENEDICT. 8030 Atherton St., Oakland 94605. (510) 562-7015. K-gr. 8.

ST. BERNARD. 1630 62nd Ave., Oakland 94621. (510) 632-6323. Fabienne Esparza, Principal. Est. 1929. Non-profit.

K-gr. 8, 210 students. $1770-$1990, sibling discounts. Reg. fee $135-$155. 65% receive fin. aid. SDH: 8:10-3. EDC: 7:10 am-6 pm; $2.50/hr., $3.50/hr. for more than one child; closed on school holidays. Avg. class size 22, max. 35; classroom aides. Uniforms. Strong academic courses in multicultural environment with caring staff. Parents contribute 20 hrs./yr. Afterschool CYO basketball. Applications taken as long as space avail. Waiting list in some grades. Two, 3 wk. summer sessions. Accredited by WASC.

"St. Bernard School provides quality, child-centered education, which is founded on gospel values. Each child is encouraged and challenged to meet their potential."

ST. COLUMBA. 1086 Alcatraz, Oakland 94608. (510) 652-2956. K-gr. 8.

ST. CYRIL. 3200 62nd Ave., Oakland 94605. (510) 638-9445. Ruby Williams, Principal. Est. 1927. Non-profit.

K-gr. 8, 210 students. $2100. Reg. fee $175. 3% receive fin. aid. SDH: 8-2:45. EDC: 7 am-6 pm, $2.50/hr., closed on school vacations. Avg. class size

20, max. 25. Uniforms. Family dinner nights, hot lunch program, drama club. Spanish for gr. 7-8. In house tutor & counselor. Afterschool basketball, girl & boy scouts. Waiting list for some grades. Parents contribute 30 hrs./yr. or pay $5/hr. Summer programs. Accredited by WASC.

"St. Cyril is committed to the spiritual, moral, and ethical development of the total child; as such we provide a strong academic program rooted in the basics."

ST. ELIZABETH. 1516 33rd Ave., Oakland 94601. (510) 532-7392. Sr. Patricia Layman, Principal; Mrs. Margarita Guevara, Admissions. Est. 1893. Non-profit.

K-gr. 8; 515 students. $2036; sibling discounts. Inc. fees $140. 20 % receive fin. aid. SDH: K, 8-11or 11:45-2:45; gr. 1-8, 8-2:35. EDC: 8 am-6 pm; $8.25/day. Avg. class size 25, max. 35; classroom aides. Uniforms. Afterschool sports for gr. 4-8. Parents contribute 30 hrs/yr. Summer programs. Accredited by WASC.

"We teach Catholic religion in a strong community. We provide opportunities for service to others and provide an overall academic curriculum."

ST. JARLATH. 2634 Pleasant St., Oakland 94602. (510) 532-4387. K-gr. 8.

ST. JOSEPH. 1910 San Antonio Ave., Alameda 94501. (510) 522-4457. Dr. Raymond L. John, Principal. Est. 1922. Non-profit.

K-gr. 8; 312 students. $3180. Inc. fees $100. 19% receive fin. aid. SDH: 8:15-2:50. EDC $2.35/hr. Avg. & max. class size 35; 3 classroom aides. Afterschool basketball, volleyball, cross country. Summer programs. Apply by May for fall placement. Children must be 5 by Oct. 1 for kdg. Accredited by WASC.

"St. Joseph exists for one reason—the total education of each student every day. Each student must receive an increase in his or her spiritual, academic, physical, and social development. This total growth can only be achieved by full participation of the students, parents, family, teachers, principal, and clergy. Each student has unique needs, abilities, and concerns, and we will strive constantly to provide an environment . . . to meet those needs."

ST. LAWRENCE O'TOOLE. 3695 High St., Oakland 94619. (510) 530-0266. Mary Maguire Pult, Principal. Est. 1951. Non-profit.

K-gr. 8; 284 students. Catholics, $2250; non-Catholics, $2730. Reg. fee $225. Fin. aid avail. SDH: K, 8:15-2; gr. 1-8, 8:15-3. EDC: 7 am-6 pm; $3/hr; closed on school holidays. Uniforms. Afterschool sports and activities. Parents required to contribute 30 hrs./yr. Testing in March for fall acceptance. Waiting list. Accredited by WASC.

"We teach the whole child; developing Catholic faith, teaching Catholic principles, promoting and modeling the love of Jesus Christ and Good News."

ST. LEO'S SCHOOL. 4238 Howe St., Oakland 94611. (510) 654-7828. Jerome DiNoto, Principal. Est. 1947. Non-profit.

PreK-gr. 8. $2500. $2300 if more than one child. Inc. fees $250. Fin. aid avail. SDH: K, 8:10-2:30; Gr. 1-8, 8:10-2:45. EDC: 7 am-6 pm; closed during school holidays. Avg. class size 25; max. 35. Aides in preK-gr. 3. Uniforms. Spanish, computers, fine arts. Afterschool basketball, volleyball, track. 20-25 hours of parent participation required. March admission testing for following year. Summer athletic camp. Accredited by WASC.

"St. Leo's provides an environment where students can learn to recognize and respect the dignity of the individual. We have a strong commitment to the spiritual, moral, ethical and academic development of the child in the context of a Christian Community."

ST. LOUIS BERTRAND. 1445—101st Ave., Oakland 94603. (510) 568-1067. Diana Adams, Principal; Karen Ellis, Admissions. Est. 1947. Non-profit.

K-gr. 8; 350 students. $2145. Inc. fees $200. No fin. aid. SDH: 8-2:30. EDC: 6:30 am-6 pm; $2.50/hr.; closed on school holidays. Avg. class size 30, max. 40; classroom aides. Dress code. Federal hot lunch program, full gym facilities, computer program. Mandatory parent participation. Afterschool basketball, track, volleyball. WASC accreditation in process.

"SLB is a student centered, family oriented school whose goal is to educate the whole individual in becoming a skilled, life-long learner ready to meet the challenges of a global, diverse community."

ST. PASCHAL BAYLON. 3710 Dorisa Ave., Oakland 94605. (510) 635-7922. K-gr. 8.

ST. PATRICK. 1630 Tenth St., Oakland 94607-1996. (510) 832-1757. K-gr. 8.

ST. PHILIP NERI. 1335 High St., Alameda 94501. (510) 521-0787. K-gr. 8.

ST. THERESA. 4850 Clarewood Dr., Oakland 94618. (510) 547-3146. K-gr. 8.

NON-CATHOLIC RELIGIOUS SCHOOLS

AGNES. 2372 E. 14th St., Oakland 94601. (510) 533-1101. K-gr. 12. Pentacostal. 25 students.

ALAMEDA CHRISTIAN. 2226 Pacific Ave., Alameda 94501. (510) 523-1000. Jean Busby, Principal. Est. 1944. Non-profit.

K-gr. 6; 50 students. K, $2280; gr. 1-6, $3480. 10% receive fin. aid. SDH: K, 8:45-11:45; gr. 1-6, 8:45-3. EDC: 7 am-6 pm; $2.50/hr.; closed on school holidays. Avg. class size 9, max. 20. Uniforms. Christian & standard text books used to form a curriculum that is thoroughly integrated with the Bible. Parent participation encouraged. Afterschool academic enrichment program.

"Alameda Christian is dedicated to training young people for Christian life and service by offering a balanced program which reflects Biblical standards. It is our purpose to educate children while supporting the spiritual priorities of the home and church."

CALVARY CHRISTIAN. 1516 Grand St., Alameda 94501. (510) 521-9695. Mary Stagnaro, Principal. Est. 1969.

K-gr. 6, 81 students. $3260, sibling discounts. Testing $20, reg. fee $24, books $45-$85. 5-10% receive fin. aid. SDH: 8-3. EDC: 6:30 am-6 pm, $62/mo., closed on school holidays. Avg. class size 11, max. 16. Uniforms. Must be 5 by 12/31 for kdg.

"We believe that parents are responsible for their child's education. We are an extension of the home, educating children spiritually, academically & physically."

CLARA MOHAMMED. 1652 47th Ave., Oakland 94601. (510) 436-7755. Islamic, K-gr. 8.

GOLDEN GATE ACADEMY. 3800 Mountain Blvd., Oakland 94619. (510) 531-0110. Seventh Day Adventist. Gr. 1-12; 200 students.

ILE OMODE. 8924 Holly St., Oakland 94621. (510) 632-8230. Okanona Ka Kalungu, Director. Est. 1986. Non-profit.

PreK-gr. 6, 56 students. $375/mo., sibling discounts. No fin. aid. SDH: 8:30-3. EDC: 7:30 am-6 pm., included in tuition. Avg. class size 10-12, max. 15. African-centered curriculum. Afterschool African drumming & dancing. Parent participation required. Summer program. Accredited by Council of Independent Black Institutes.

"Ile Omode School is an Educational Institution of Wo'se Community Church of the African Way. . . Our goal is to create a learning environment which encourages creative problem solving, teamwork, and confidence. Through learning experiences that are both challenging and fun, we arc preparing our children to compete in a technologically advanced society. We emphasize African values and community as a framework for the utilization of this technology. . .We stress the development of our students' bodies, minds, souls, and consciousness. . ."

NORTHERN LIGHT. 4500 Redwood Rd., Oakland 94619. (510)530-9366. Nance A. Tovar, Director. K-gr. 7.

OAKLAND HEBREW DAY. 215 Ridgeway Ave., Oakland 94611. (510) 652-4324. M. Cohen, Director. Est. 1992. Non-profit.

K-gr. 4. K, $5400; gr. 1-4, $5950. $200 materials fee. 25% receive fin. aid. SDH: K, 8:30-2; gr. 1-3, 8:30-3:30; gr. 4, 8:15-3:45. EDC: 2-6 pm, $4.25/hr., open on school vacations. Avg. class size 12-16, max. 16. Dress code. Modern Hebrew language and Jewish studies; through art, music, and stories, students learn about Jewish holidays, traditions and values. Apply by Feb. 15; one parent must be Jewish; kdg. readiness screening; waiting list.

"O.H.D.S. is a modern Orthodox co-educational Jewish day school in which Jewish values and practices form the centerpiece. . . It offers an integrated, developmental curriculum in a hands-on, whole language environment. We are committed to academic excellence in both general and Jewish studies."

OPERATION KICK-OFF. 6118 E. 14th St., Oakland 94612. (510) 568-3333. Christian, K-gr. 3.

PATTEN ACADEMY. 2433 Coolidge Ave., Oakland 94601. (510) 533-3121; 533-8300. Dr. Evelyn Swanson, Principal. Est. 1944. Non-profit.

K-gr. 12; 220 students. K, $1725; gr. 1-8, $2175; gr. 9-12, $2775. Inc. fees K, $335; gr. 1-8, $350; gr. 9-12, $450 (includes text books). Sibling discounts. 5% receive fin. aid. SDH: K, 8:30-12:30; gr. 1-6, 8:30-3; gr. 7-8, 8:45-3:30; gr. 9-12, 8:45-4. Avg. class size 20, max. 25; classroom aides. Uniforms. Full and varied academic program combining three components: excellence in general studies, development of the Christian experience and values, and enrichment through music, computer education, Bible instruction, foreign languages and field trips. Parent service hours encouraged. May apply any time. Waiting list. Accredited by WASC.

"The Patten Academy of Christian Education (PACE) embraces an educational ideal bringing together the finest in contemporary educational experiences in an atmosphere reflective of Jesus Christ. The fundamental aim is to encourage each child's intellectual, social, creative, and spiritual development. From this harmonious development, PACE students derive an abiding enthusiasm for learning."

PENTACOSTAL WAY OF TRUTH. 1575 Seventh St., Oakland 94607. (510) 835-7866. K-gr. 12, 52 students.

ST. ANDREW MISSIONARY BAPTIST. 2624 West St., Oakland 94612. (510) 465-8023. K-gr. 12, 265 students.

ST. PAUL'S EPISCOPAL. 116 Montecito Ave., Oakland 94610. (510) 287-9600. FAX: (510) 832-3231. Richard Ackerly, Headmaster. Kit Land, Admissions. Est. 1975. Non-profit.

K-gr. 8; 242 students. $1375-$8750, sliding scale tuition. $50 application fee.
39% receive fin. aid. SDH: K, 8:30-2:30; gr. 1-6, 8:30-3; gr. 7-8, 8:30-3:30.
EDC avail. on school holidays. Avg. & max. class size 22; teaching assistants
& specialists; teacher-student ratio 1:11.5. Swimming, drama, music,
drumming. Spanish, art, music, computer & P.E. taught by specialists. The
school takes advantage of its central city location to use the city's parks,
museums, & libraries and to implement its community service program. Apply
by Jan. 15; must be 5 by Sept. 1 for kdg. Waiting list. Single parents contribute
15 hrs./yr; 2 parent families contribute 30 hrs./yr. Most diverse study body &
faculty of any independent school in the Bay Area. Every student involved in
award-winning community service program. 95% of grads accepted at 1st
choice high school. Afterschool classes & team sports. Summer programs.
Accredited by WASC & CAIS.

"St. Paul's is . . .a community that celebrates and values diversity. . .and seeks
to reflect that of its city and region. . .St. Paul's measures its academic
excellence in achievement. . .and also in the development of independent
thinking, intellectual curiosity, self-confidence and positive relations with
others. . .St. Paul's is in the Episcopal tradition of ecumenical school and church
working together to teach both academics and human values in a compassionate
environment, offering a program appropriate to children of all faiths. . ."

ZION LUTHERAN. 5201 Park Blvd., Piedmont 94611. (510) 530-7909.
Alberta Strelow, Principal. Est. 1883. Non-profit.

K-gr. 8; 183 students. $3250. No fin. aid. SDH: 8:40-3. EDC: 7am-6 pm;
$3/hr; closed during school holidays. Avg. class size 20, max., 25. Aides in
some classes. Uniforms. Annual worship dramas or operettas. Each class
prepares one chapel a year. Afterschool basketball, softball, volleyball. Annual
track meet for all grades. Parents serve 20 hrs./yr. Waiting list. Accredited by
WASC; in process of NLSA accreditation.

"One of the most precious gifts God has given us is the gift of children It is our
goal to provide a school where parents may leave their children during the day,
secure that the children will receive proper Christian influence and examples,
supervision, individual guidance, and the best in elementary education. "

SECULAR SCHOOLS

ARCHWAY. 250 41st St., Oakland 94611. (510) 547-4747. Lois Foster,
Director. Est. 1973. Non-profit.

K-gr. 8, 65 students. $5250-$5650. Inc. fees $300. 30% receive fin. aid.
SDH: K-gr. 2, 9-2; gr. 4-8, 8:45-3. EDC: full-time, $1800-$2400; pm only,
$1500-$1800; closed on school holidays. Avg. class size 10, max. 12-18; aides
in some classes. Dress code. Science, math lab, field trips, cooking and

diversified arts. Art studio staffed by art teacher, instruction in pottery, painting, stained glass. Various enrichment specialists incorporated into the program. Should apply by Feb. 1 but enrollment remains open as long as space is avail. For kdg. should be 5 by Sept. but exceptions are made. Afterschool program for K-gr. 6, older children go to the YMCA. Summer Programs: Science Explorations (ages 6-9); Cuisine & Art (ages 10-14).

"Archway approaches learning with an academically challenging curriculum which is personalized, balanced, and effective. Hands-on, relevant activities are intrinsic to our instructional mode. We value children's natural curiosity. Our small school setting encourages trust and openness with peers and staff— qualities we consider essential to wholesome moral growth."

AURORA. 40 Dulwich Rd., Oakland 94618. (510) 428-2606. Bob Whitlow, Director. Est. 1988. Non-profit.

K-gr. 6, 110 students. $5500-$6600. Inc. fees $300. 15% receive fin. aid. SDH: K-gr. 3, 8:45-2:20; gr. 4-6, 8:45-3:30. EDC: 7:45 am-6 pm, $200/mo.; open on school holidays. Avg. class size 18, max. 24; classroom aides. Specialists teach music, art, computers, Spanish. Active parent participation. Afterschool activities vary: karate, chess, art, gardening, music. Admissions based on interviews, no entrance tests; open to LD students; waiting list. Summer science & drama programs.

Aurora is a multi-graded school based on hands-on learning and an integrated curriculum. The school follows the California curriculum frameworks and utilizes authentic assessments and the whole language approach to reading and writing.

BEACON DAY. 2101 Livingston St., Oakland 94606. (510) 436-4466. Thelma A. Farley, Director of Education; Aubyn Boyer, Admissions. Est. 1982. Non-profit.

Preschool-gr. 8; 285 students. $575/mo. (school day); $775 (w/EDC). Bldg. fee $350-500. 10% receive fin. aid. SDH: 8:30-3. EDC: 7:30 am-6 pm, open year-round. Avg. class size 15, max. 19; classroom aides. 5 hrs. of arts instruction/wk, dance & vocal ensemble. Specialists teach computer, Spanish, motor skills, music, dance, art. On site L.D. specialist. Afterschool intramural & competitive sports for older students. Year-round placements, monthly open house. School accepts students with a wide range of learning styles & needs.

"Beacon Day School—a thriving, diverse school community—offers a year-round developmental program to children from 3-13 yrs. Children are grouped into non-graded classrooms where the focus is hands-on, group learning."

BENTLEY. 1 Hiller Dr., Oakland 94618. (510) 843-2512. Robert A. Munro, Headmaster. Pat Finlayson, Admissions. Est. 1920. Non-profit.

K-gr. 8, 300 students. $8900-$9300. Books & field trips, extra. Fin. aid avail. SDH: K, 8:30-3:30; gr. 1-8, 8:30-3:30. EDC: 7:30 am-6 pm; cost included in tuition; closed on school holidays. 4 acre campus in residential area of Hiller Highlands. Avg. class size 18, max. 20; interns help in the classrooms. Specialists teach art, music, foreign languages, P.E., performing arts. Afterschool team & recreational sports, arts & crafts, sewing. Accredited by CAIS.

"Bentley School provides a strong academic program in the areas of English, math, social studies, science, and foreign language. The program is enriched with art, music, performing arts, computers, & physical education classes. The school provides a nurturing and stable learning environment."

THE CHILD UNIQUE MONTESSORI. 2226 Encinal Ave., Alameda 94501. (510) 521-9227. Veronica Ufoegbune, Director; Dierde Imara, Admissions. Est. 1983.

18 mos.-gr. 8. $483-$513; full day, $649. SDH: K, 8:45-2:45; gr. 1-3, 8:30-2:30; gr. 4-8, 8:20-3. EDC: 7 am-6 pm, $3/hr.; open on school holidays. Avg. class size 10, max. 15-18; classroom aides. Specialists teach math, history, health & art. Parents contribute 30 hrs./yr. Apply any time. Summer programs. Accredited by PACE.

"Beginning in preschool, a child's desire to learn becomes a springboard for the reception of unlimited knowledge. Children learn at a level commensurate with their ability and desire. Child Unique teachers open up a world of geography, history, music, and the sciences to enhance a child's potential for growth. The school emphasizes the connection between living and learning. Older students work in the community and maintain a bank account; younger ones start community gardens and write books and plays."

GARNER PRIMARY. 2152 Central Ave., Alameda 94501. (510) 522-0404. K-gr. 2.

THE HEAD-ROYCE SCHOOL. 4315 Lincoln Ave., Oakland 94602. (510) 531-1300. Paul D. Chapman, Headmaster. Luzanne Engh, Admissions. Est. 1887. Non-profit.

K-gr. 12; 700 students (250 in K-gr. 6; 150 in gr. 7-8; 300 in gr. 9-12.) K-gr. 8, $7600-$10,950; gr. 9-12, $11,400. Inc. fees $90-$600. 12% receive fin. aid. SDH:: K, 8:25-2; gr. 1-8, 8:25-3:20. EDC: 7:45-8:30 am (no fee); 8:25-3:20 ($1425/yr); closed on school holidays. Avg. class size 15; max. 18 in K-gr. 8, 16 in gr. 9-12; classroom aides in kdg. & gr. 1. 14 acre campus includes computer lab, music/performance studio, soccer field, baseball diamond, basketball & tennis courts, swimming pool, extended care room. Specialists teach art, music, P.E., computer, foreign language, library. On-site L.D. specialist. Weekly assemblies, chorus, newspaper, community service projects. Spanish & French begin in gr. 4. Latin also avail. in gr.7-8. Wilderness trips &

variety of high-interest, non-graded electives offered in middle school. Afterschool sports for gr. 7-12. Parents contribute 16 hrs./yr. Apply by Dec. for fall entrance in K-gr. 8. Must be 5 by 9/1 for kdg. Waiting list. Summer enrichment program for K-gr. 8. Accredited by WASC & CAIS.

Gr. 9-12: Open campus. Ability grouping in math & foreign languages. Art & computer labs, photo & video studios; senior projects; accelerated programs at UCB. 13 AP classes. French, Spanish, Latin, Japanese. Strong fine arts & athletic programs. College counselor. 100% of grads. attend 4 yr. colleges. SAT scores (100%): Class of '94, V 613, M 656; '93, V 590, M 607. Open house & school visits Oct.-Jan; testing Dec.-Feb.; apply by mid-Jan. Waiting list.

"Head-Royce offers a challenging and exciting educational program that seeks to develop intellectual abilities; to foster in each student integrity, self-esteem, compassion and a sense of humor; to nurture aesthetic abilities; and to promote social responsibility and encourage healthy living and physical fitness."

HORIZON PRESCHOOL AND PRIMARY. 9520 Mountain Blvd., Oakland 94605. (510) 635-7470. K-gr. 3.

MILLS COLLEGE CHILDREN'S SCHOOL. 5000 MacArthur Blvd., Oakland 94613. (510) 430-2118. Joan Henry, Director. Est. 1926. Non-profit.

Infants-gr. 3; 42 children in K-gr. 3. $5350/yr. 6-7% receive fin. aid. SDH: 9-2. EDC: 2-3:30 ($1,000/yr.) or 2-5:15 ($2166/yr); closed on school holidays. Avg. class size 20, max. 21. Mills College students working towards education degrees serve as classroom aides. Students placed in multi-aged classes and stay with a teacher for more than one year. Dramatic play, art, music and dance; emphasis on creativity rather than imitation. Mathematics part of daily classroom living with emphasis on manipulative materials and real life situations. Science emphasis on "learning by doing." Early enrollment in Jan. & Feb. Remaining spots filled March-July. Priority given to children of Mills' students, staff and faculty as long as balanced, ethnically diverse classrooms can be maintained. No admissions testing but parents must agree with school's philosophy. Waiting list. Three, one month summer sessions 9-5.

"We encourage independent thinking and foster our children's sense of discovery because children need to be partners in the learning process. Children have choices and our child-centered curriculum evolves from the children's interests. . . The Children's School is a lab school for the Department of Education at Mills College. Its primary purpose is to provide a classroom laboratory to educate early childhood professionals."

MONTESSORI CASA DEI BAMBINI. 281 Santa Clara Ave., Oakland. (510) 836-4313. Helen Sears, Director. Est. 1978. Non-profit.

Preschool-gr. 6. Kdg. am, $5060, full day, $5540; gr. 1-6, $5710. Inc. fees $375. 5% receive fin. aid. SDH: K, 8:30-1 or 8:30-2:45; gr. 1-6, 8:30-2:45.

EDC: 7:30-am-6 pm; $3.25/hr; open on school holidays. Avg. class size 13, max. 20. Each class has a full-time Montessori Guide & a teaching assistant. Children work individually & in small groups. Spanish & gymnastics classes. Drama, computers, foreign languages, library skills. Week long music & drama workshop. Environmental ed. trip. Summer day camp for kdg.; 2 wk. opera program for gr. 1-6. Elementary program open to children with no previous Montessori experience. Apply by mid-March. Parents contribute 15 hrs./yr.

We "present concepts in relation to an overview, and to one another in an interconnected curriculum and build from the concrete to the abstract. Rather than teaching rules or concepts to memorize, the classroom provides tools for discovering the rules...we encourage critical thinking and reasoning and promote group awareness and empathy. Group activities and accomplishments lead to respect for the contributions of others, a willingness to help, tolerance for individual differences and doing one's best in a common effort."

OAKLAND MONTESSORI. 3625 Fruitvale, Oakland 94602. (510) 482-3111. PreK-gr. 3; 25 students in K-gr. 3.

PARK DAY. 370 43rd St., Oakland 94609-2223. (510) 653-0317. Tom Little, Director. Flo Hodes, Admissions. Est. 1976. Non-profit.

K-gr. 6, 224 students. $6300. 20% receive fin. aid. SDH: K & gr.1, 9-2:45, gr. 2-6, 9-3. EDC: 7:30 am-6 pm, cost varies. 14-18 students/teacher. Campus on two acres in park-like setting. Spanish for all grades, computers, performing arts. Specialists teach Spanish, art, movement. Gardening Society, Day of Sharing, weekly songfests where students may perform solo or in groups. Parents contribute 25 hrs./yr. Afterschool sports, drama, art. School welcomes students with diverse learning styles; on site L.D. specialist paid for by parents. Parents should begin application process in Nov. Students visit Jan-Feb. No academic testing; acceptance based on visit & interview and on school's desire to have economic, racial & ethnic diversity in the student body; for kdg. child must be 5 by Sept. 1. Independent arts camp in summer.

"Park Day School parents and staff believe a school can provide quality education in an atmosphere that reflects the natural curiosity of children and their diverse learning styles. . . Hands-on, ears-on, eyes-on, minds-on activities are central to an educational program. . . Being curious, verbalizing questions, exploring possibilities, learning from mistakes, using information already acquired—these are all elements of the learning process and are necessary for children to function creatively and intelligently in problem solving."

PETER PAN ACADEMY. 3171 Macartney Rd., Alameda 94502. (510) 523-4080. K-gr. 6, 100 students.

REDWOOD DAY SCHOOL. 3245 Sheffield Ave., Oakland 94602. (510) 534-0800. Joel Rosenberg, Director. Est. 1962. Non-profit.

Jr. K- gr. 8; 160 students. $6900-$7975. Inc. fees $375. 20-25% receive fin. aid. SDH: Jr. K- gr. 1, 8:30-3:10; gr. 2-5, 8:30-3:15; gr. 6-8, 8:15-3:20. EDC:7:45 am-6 pm; $175/mo; open on school holidays. Avg. class size 18-20, max. 22. Aides in Jr. K-gr. 2. Transportation to Alameda. Dress code. Full gymnasium, auditorium, pool on 3.5 acres in quiet residential area. Specialists teach art, music, computers, P.E., Spanish & French. Parent participation encouraged. Afterschool activities: study hall 4 days/wk; flag football, basketball, volleyball, softball for gr. 5-8; variety of other activities. Apply by end of Feb. Waiting list in some grades. Full summer program includes swimming. Accredited by CAIS.

"Redwood Day School balances a strong academic program with a nurturing social environment and personal support through small classes and quality teachers. Ethnic and socio-economic diversity contribute greatly to the special warmth and good feelings of the student body and parent community. The home-school partnership assures individual attention and understanding for all students."

RISING STAR MONTESSORI. 1421 High St., Alameda 94501. (510) 865-4536. Ann Garvey, Owner. Est. 1982. Proprietary.

K-gr. 3; 50 students. $425-$440/mo. Materials fee $50-$150. No fin. aid. SDH: 8:30-3. EDC: 7 am-6 pm; $3.50/hr.; open on school holidays. Avg. class size 20, max. 26; teacher/student ratio 1:12; classroom aides. 10 wk. summer school; 2 wks. extended care. Parents contribute 12 hrs. or $100 extra. Applicants accepted year-round after half day visit, 2 wk. probation. Accredited by AMS.

Rising Star provides "a Montessori setting where children learn more at their own pace with teachers as leaders."

Castro Valley ◆ San Leandro ◆ San Lorenzo

CATHOLIC SCHOOLS

ASSUMPTION. 1851 136th Ave., San Leandro 94578. (510) 357-8772. Mrs. Jean Schroeder, Principal. Est. 1952. Non-profit.

K-gr. 8, 285 students. $2229 (in parish), reg. fee $195, fund-raising $400. 10% receive fin. aid. SDH: K, 8:05-12 or 10:45-2:45; gr. 1-8, 8:05-2:45. EDC: noon-6 pm; closed on school holidays. Avg. class size 33, max. 35; 3 classroom aides. Uniforms. Music classes, annual musicals, library facility, extended day care facility. School psychologist assesses students with learning disabilities. Afterschool basketball, drama, participation in city activities (e.g., carolling & Cherry Festival). Parents contribute 30 hrs./yr. to school. All new students are accepted on academic & behavioral probation for at least the 1st year. Accredited by WASC.

"Christianity is integrated into every facet of a child's educational experience and enables the student to become more fully developed, free to think, love and reach out to the greater community."

OUR LADY OF GRACE. 19920 Anita Ave., Castro Valley 94546. (510) 581-3155. K-gr. 8, 300 students.

ST. FELICITAS. 1650 Manor Blvd., San Leandro 94579. (510) 357-2530. K-gr. 8.

ST. JOACHIM. 21250 Hesperian, Blvd., Hayward 94541. (510) 783-3177. K-gr. 8, 315 students. EDC avail.

ST. JOHN. 270 E. Lewelling Blvd., San Lorenzo 94580. (510) 276-6632.

ST. LEANDER YEAR ROUND SCHOOL. 451 Davis St., San Leandro 94577-2746. (510) 351-4144. Joyce E. Braun, Principal. Est. 1881. Non-profit.

Pre K-gr. 8, 270 students. $2475, sibling discounts. Reg. fee $175. 5% receive fin. aide. SDH: Pre K, 12:45-2:45; K, 8:05-11:35; gr. 1-8, 8:05-2:45. EDC: 6:45 am-6 pm; $2.50/hr; closed on school holidays. Avg. class size 27, max. 32. Aides in primary grades. Dress code. Specialists teach computer, instrumental & choral music, P.E. Art & Spanish to gr. 6-8. On-site tutor for L.D. students. Gym & auditorium. Computer club, honor chorus for gr. 6-8, children's chorus for gr. 3-5. Afterschool CYO basketball, field & track. Parents required to help at non-smoking Bingo games and contribute 20 hrs/yr. (10 hrs. for single parents.) Applications & testing in March; waiting list in some grades. For Kdg., child must be 5 by Oct. 1. 180 day school year begins 1st wk. of Aug, ends mid-June. Accredited by WASC & WCEA.

"St. Leander strives to teach and model the 'good news' as revealed by Jesus Christ—in particular, a respect for all life and the dignity of each person, recognizing the beauty of diversity in individuals, cultures, and traditions. With parent involvement, we provide quality education in a safe, nurturing environment conducive to learning."

NON-CATHOLIC RELIGIOUS SCHOOLS

CALVARY LUTHERAN. 17200 Via Magdalena, San Lorenzo 94580. (510) 278-9640. Forrest Adams, Principal. Est. 1950. Non-profit.

Preschool-gr. 8. 4% receive fin. aid. SDH: K, 8:30-11:30; gr. 1-8, 8:30-3. EDC: 7 am-6 pm; $2.10/hr.; open on school holidays. Avg. & max. class size 26. Dress code. Interscholastic sports for gr. 7-8.

"Our goal is to prepare the whole child by teaching Christian values and morals, academics, respect and self-discipline in a loving environment."

CHINESE CHRISTIAN. 750 Fargo Ave., San Leandro 94579. (510) 351-4957; FAX, (510) 351-1789. Raymond Ng, Superintendent. Est. 1978. Non-profit.

K-gr 12; 750 students. $3100, sibling discounts. Reg. $100, admissions testing $100. 15% receive fin. aid. SDH: 8:30 am-3:15: EDC: 7 am-4 pm, no charge; 4-6 pm, $60/mo. 13 school buses provide fee based transportation. Uniforms. Avg. & max. class size: K, 26; gr. 1-12, 28. 20 aides, one always present in K-gr. 2. 9.5 acre campus, 32 classrooms, library w/ over 7000 volumes & staff librarian, CD-rom research capability, video library. Extensive athletic facilities. Cantonese in K-gr. 8; Mandarin in gr. 9-12. Classes for Chinese-speaking students w/ limited English proficiency. Comprehensive Bible-based curriculum including Bible, music & art. Award winning Marching units, school newspaper & yearbook. School participates in many academic, artistic, & athletic competitions. Jr. & Senior High: college prep, AP classes, college counselor, computer science, visual & performing arts. Applications accepted up to 2 yrs. in advance. Waiting list in most grades.

"Chinese Christian School is an educational ministry of the Bay Area Chinese Bible Church and . . . is dedicated to providing high academics with an emphasis on Christian character to the Chinese and Asian community in the Bay Area."

COMMUNITY CHRISTIAN SCHOOL. 562 Lewelling Blvd., San Leandro. 94579. (510) 351-3684. Susan McCarrie, Principal. Est. 1990. Non-profit.

K-gr. 8; 172 students. $2750. Reg. fee, $100-$125. 28% receive fin. aid. SDH:8:30-3. EDC: 7 am-6 pm; $2/hr; open on school holidays. Avg. class size 23, max. 40 with 2 teachers. Classroom aides. Uniforms. Support missions, basketball league, "United in Son" Festival, Christmas Program. Computers for gr. 6-8, sign language for gr. 7-8, Yearbook Club. A Beka curriculum. Encourage parent participation. Afterschool basketball and yearbook club. Waiting list for some grades. Must be 5 by 12/31 for kdg.

We "offer children and their parents a school which is well grounded in academic and social growth based on sound biblical principles; a school where children feel at home away from home and parents feel secure in the atmosphere and teaching their children receive."

REDWOOD CHRISTIAN SCHOOLS. (Mailing address) 4200 James Ave., Castro Valley 94546. (510) 889-7526. Bruce D. Johnson, Sr., Superintendent. Est. 1970. Non-profit.

K-gr. 12. 900+ students. K-gr. 6, $4297; gr. 7-8, $4813; gr. 9-12, $5175 Sibling discounts. Inc. fees $100. 20% receive fin. aid. SDH: K-gr. 6, 9-3:30; gr. 7-12, 8:20-2:40. EDC: 7 am-6 pm, open all year. 2 elem. campuses in Castro Valley, 1 jr.-sen high campus in San Leandro. Avg. class size 25. Max. class size: K-gr. 6, 30; gr. 7-12, 32. Aides in some classes. Teacher-student ratio no more than 1:9, usually 1:6 or 7. Bus service available. Dress code.

PEACH (providing extra attention care & hope) program for K-gr.6. Interscholastic sports for gr. 4-12; 8 sports in gr. 7-8; 15 sports for gr. 9-12. Curriculum specialists for all grades. Parent participation voluntary but highly encouraged. Students may enroll year round. Waiting list. Pull-out program for L.D. students. Summer programs: day camp, day care, and academic day care. Accredited by ASCI & WASC.

"RCS is an interdenominational, independent Christian school built on Christian truth, high academics, pure morals, patriotism & self-discipline being taught and modeled to our students. We are committed to Christian truth and becoming partners with Christian parents and non-Christian parents open to Christian teachings at home, church, and school."

SECULAR SCHOOLS

CAMELOT. 2330 Pomar Vista, Castro Valley 94546. (510) 481-1304. Georgina Meehan, Administrator. Est. 1978. Proprietary.

Infants-gr. 6; 115 students in K-gr. 6. K & 1st, $100/wk; gr. 2-6, $95/wk. Reg. fee $50; curriculum fee $135-$195. 5% receive fin. aid. SDH: K, 8:45-12:15; gr. 1-6, 8:30-3. EDC included in tuition, open on school holidays. Avg. class size 17, max. 24. Classroom aides if K over 15, gr. 1-4 over 18. Spacious campus with divided play areas and large field & full basketball court. Multi-cultural education. Spanish. Outdoor ed. camp for gr. 6. Breakfast, snack & lunch program. Dance, computer instruction and tutoring available . Optional study hall. Parents encouraged to assist in classrooms, field trips, parties etc. Afterschool clubs in sports, cooking, science, arts & crafts, roller skating, nature study etc. offered on rotating basis. 11 wk. summer camp. Fall reg. in March. Waiting list.

"Camelot's experienced staff and small classes provide children with the opportunity to reach their potential. Our program is challenging and creative, and is designed to encourage both critical and logical thought."

MONTESSORI SCHOOL OF SAN LEANDRO. 16292 Foothill Blvd., San Leandro. (510) 278-1115. Dr. Pamela Lanaro, Director. Est. 1980. Non-profit.

K-gr. 6; 150 students. $3500. Technology fee $250, books $200. SDH: 8:30-3. EDC: 7 am-6 pm, $100/mo. Avg. class size 25, max. 35. Reading specialist. Daily Spanish; Latin for upper elementary. Specialists teach art, music, Spanish dance. Music room, five computers in each classroom, large soccer field. LD students are tested and work with specialist. Apply by April 1. Afterschool boy and girl scout troops, daily PE 3-4. Accredited by American Montessori Society.

"The child self-constructs knowledge through an individualized program which emphasizes manipulative and multi-media exploration. A rich science and mathematics program is complimented with an equally rich arts program."

Fremont ◆ Hayward ◆ Newark ◆ Union City

CATHOLIC SCHOOLS

ALL SAINTS. 22870 Second St., Hayward 94541. (510) 582-1910. Marilyn Marchi, Principal. K-gr. 8, 310 students.

HOLY SPIRIT. 3930 Parish Ave., Fremont 94536. (510) 793-3553. Dr. James T. Brennan, Principal. Est. 1961. Non-profit.

K-gr. 8; 380 students. $2580. Reg. fee $180. SDH: 8-3. EDC: $3/hr., closed on school holidays. Avg. class size 38, max. 40; 4 aides. Uniforms. Science & computer labs. Afterschool CYO sports. Parents contribute 40 hrs./yr. Apply between Jan. 15 & March 15; waiting list. Summer programs. Accredited by WASC.

OUR LADY OF THE ROSARY. 678 B Street, Union City 94587. (510) 471-3765. Yolanda Szilagyi, Principal. (510) 471-3765. Est. 1967. Non-profit.

K-gr. 8; 140 students. $2290-$3490; sibling discounts. Reg. fee $170; testing fee $30. No scholarships. SDH: 8-3. EDC: 7 am-6 pm, closed on school holidays. Avg. class size 25, max. 30; two classroom aides. Uniforms. Computer lab for K-gr. 4; IBM computers in gr. 5-8. Reading specialist for gr. 1; math/science specialist for gr. 8. Afterschool CYO sports. Families contribute 15-30 hrs./yr. Apply in Feb. & March; must be 4 yrs. 10 mos. by Sept. 1 for kdg. Summer school in June & July.

ST. BEDE. 26910 Patrick Ave., Hayward 94544. (510) 782-3444. Madeleine M. De La Fontaine, Principal. Est. 1964. Non-profit.

K-gr. 8; 220 students. $240/mo. Reg. fee, $165. SDH: 8:10-2:50. EDC: 7 am-6:30 p.m. $3/hr.; closed on school holidays. Avg. & max. class size 35. Aides in some classes. Uniforms. Full range of extra-curricular activities: sports, drama, choir & more. 2 gyms, playing fields. Some modifications made for L.D. students. Apply by March 15. Accredited by WCEA.

"Jesus Christ and the gospel values he taught are the foundation of our philosophy. Parents are primary educators and we assist them as we strive to develop and educate the whole child."

ST. CLEMENT. 790 Calhoun St., Hayward 94544. (510) 538-5885. K-gr. 8.

ST. EDWARD. P.O. Box 245, Newark 94560. (510) 793-7242. K-gr. 8.

ST. JOSEPH. 43222 Mission Blvd., Fremont 94539. (510) 656-6525. Sr. Barbara Hagel, O. P., Principal. Est. 1960. Non-profit.

Gr. 1-8; 283 students. $2270, sibling discounts. Reg. fee $90. 2% receive fin. aid. SDH: 8:15-3. EDC: $2.75-$3.25/hr. Avg. & max. class size 35; classroom aides. Art history program for all grades, computer ed., P.E., library, whole language, math/science nucleus. School counselor, part-time music teacher, student govt., yearbook. 6th grade science camp, field trips, Ohlone Week for gr. 6-8, D.A.R.E, liturgical celebrations. Afterschool CYO softball, basketball, volleyball, track. Parents contribute 40 hrs./yr. Apply by late March. Accredited by WASC.

"St. Joseph School strives to aid children in the development of Christian values, academic growth and good citizenship. The education program is directed toward growth of the whole person: spiritual, intellectual, social, and physical being."

ST. LEONARD. 3635 St. Leonard's Way, Fremont 94538. (510) 657-1674. Sister Carmel Marie, O.P., Principal. Est. 1964. Non-profit.

K-gr. 8, 300 students. In parish, $2450; out-of-parish, $2850. Sibling discounts. Inc. fees $195. Fin. aid avail. SDH: 8-2:50. EDC: 8 am-6 pm. Avg. class size 32-35, max. 35; classroom aides. Uniforms. Music, art. Hot lunch once a week. Afterschool CYO sports. Dual parent families contribute 30 hrs./yr; single parents 15 hrs./yr. Waiting list. Accredited by WASC.

". . .At St. Leonard we believe that the multi-ethnic and multi-cultural diversity of our students fosters understanding and caring. We help each individual discover his/her own giftedness and support the development of a healthy self-concept. We believe that the positive development of mind, body, and soul will instill the desire to serve God by serving others. St. Leonard School community promotes a fundamental spirit of respect and service on the part of the students, parents, and staff."

NON-CATHOLIC RELIGIOUS SCHOOLS

AMERICAN HERITAGE CHRISTIAN. 425 Gresel St., Hayward 94544. (510) 471-1010. K-gr. 12.

BAYSIDE SEVENTH-DAY ADVENTIST CHRISTIAN. 26400 Gading Rd., Hayward 94544. (510) 785-1313. Jim Winters, Principal. Est. 1962. Non-profit.

K-gr. 8, 65 students. $2250. Reg. fee $185. Discounts avail., but no scholarships. SDH: K, 8:30-12; gr. 1-8, 8:30-3:15 (2:00 on Fri.). EDC: until 5:30 or 6 pm, $2.75-$3/hr, closed on school holidays. Dress code. Avg. class size 15, max. 20. Bible classes in all grades. Field trips, assemblies, computer instruction. No transfers accepted after Dec. 15. Accredited by North American Division of Seventh Day Adventists.

"We welcome the interest of any parent of any boy or girl who desires a character-building education. To accomplish the high aims of Christian education, it is of utmost importance that full cooperation exist between the home, teacher, & students."

CALVARY BAPTIST. 41354 Roberts Ave., Fremont 94538. (510) 656-5311. K-gr. 12, 30 students.

CHRISTIAN COMMUNITY. 39700 Mission Blvd., Fremont 94539. (510) 651-KIDS. Jeneane Stevens, Principal. Est. 1980. Non-profit.

Preschool-gr. 8; 445 students. Fin. aid avail. SDH: 8:30-3. EDC: 7 am-6 pm, avail. on school holidays. Avg. class size 25-28, max. 28; classroom aides. Uniforms. Computer lab, music, drama, Bible, new gym. Afterschool sports for gr. 6-8. Parents contribute 10 hrs./yr. Apply in early spring. Waiting list for some grades. All day summer program. School considering adding a program for L.D. students. Accredited by ACSI.

"The cornerstone of our education is the Bible, which is used to support the family in teaching strong moral values, character, and discipline. Supplementing this is a diverse academic program designed to be enriching, relevant, and rewarding."

CHRISTIAN HERITAGE ACADEMY. 36060 Fremont Blvd., Fremont 94536. (510) 797-7938. K-gr. 12, 120 students.

FREMONT CHRISTIAN. 4760 Thorton Ave., Fremont 94536. (510) 792-4700. K-gr. 12.

KINGS ACADEMY. 38325 Cedar Blvd., Newark 94560. (510) 793-8001. K-gr. 12.

LANDMARK BAPTIST. 573 Bartlett Ave., Hayward 94541. (510) 785-2166. K-gr. 12.

LEA'S CHRISTIAN SCHOOL. 26236 Adrian Ave., Hayward 94545. (510) 785-2477. Janet Yoshida, Director. Est. 1978. Non-profit.

K-gr. 4, 85 students. $2550, sibling discounts. $145 reg. fee, $25 field trips. No fin. aid. SDH: 9-3. EDC: 7 am-3:30, $2.50/hr., closed on school holidays. Avg. class size 20, max. 22; aides. Dress code. Families contribute 15 hrs. of service/yr; parents also required to monitor homework. Waiting list. Students with learning disabilities given individualized instruction and attention within classroom. Six. wk. summer program.

"Our goal is to provide a loving environment in which young children may grow physically, spiritually, emotionally and intellectually. We stress the development of a positive self-image in each child. We believe that children who learn to love and respect themselves in their early years will maintain an enthusiasm for learning and a concern for their fellow man in their future years."

MISSION HILLS CHRISTIAN. 225 Driscoll Rd., Fremont 94539. (510) 490-7709. Est. 1963. Non-profit.

K-gr. 8, 37 students. K, $2070; gr. 1-8, $2670. Reg. fee $175. 1% receive fin. aid. SDH: K, 8-11:30; gr. 1, 8-1; gr. 2-4, 8-3; gr. 5-8, 8-3:15. EDC: after school until 6 pm, $2.75/hr., closed on school holidays. Dress code.

"The small size of our school allows us to know each child individually and develop an understanding of each child. Daily Bible study provides each child with the opportunity to question and develop an understanding of Christian beliefs and morals and the value of each individual in the creator's eyes."

PRINCE OF PEACE LUTHERAN. 38451 Fremont Blvd., Fremont 94536. (510) 797-8186. Robert Marty, Principal. Est. 1957. Non-profit.

K-gr. 8; 190 students. $1230-$3140. Reg. fee $200. 10% receive fin. aid. SDH: K, 8:30-11:30 or 12-3; gr. 1-8, 8:30-3. EDC: 7 am-6 pm; $2.20/hr.; open on school holidays. Dress code. Avg. class size 24, max. 28; classroom aides. Parents contribute 18-35 hrs./yr. Afterschool volleyball, basketball, track. Accredited by Natl. Lutheran School Assoc. & WASC.

We "assist parents in their responsibility of educating the whole child."

THE SUNSHINE SCHOOL. 20625 Garden Ave., Hayward 94541. (510) 293-0300. K-gr. 8.

SECULAR SCHOOLS

CAMELOT. 21753 Vallejo St., Hayward 94541. (510) 581-5125. Georgina Meehan, Administrator. Est. 1978. Proprietary.

Preschool-gr. 1 (students can continue on through gr. 6 at Castro Valley campus). 32 students in Kdg. & gr. 1. $100/wk. Reg. fee $50; curriculum fee: K, $135: gr. 1, $185. 5% receive fin. aid. SDH: K, 8:30-12:15; gr. 1, 8:30-3. EDC included in tuition, open on school holidays. Avg. class size 16; max. 24 in K, 20 in 1st. Aide in K if over 15 students, in 1st if over 18. Tree shaded campus with a variety of equipment. Spanish in 1st gr. Computer and dance. Tutoring avail. Multi-cultural curriculum; breakfast, snacks & lunch program. Variety of programs offered after school. Parents encouraged to help in classrooms, field trips, parties etc. 11 wk. summer camp for K-gr.2. Register in March for fall placement.

"In kindergarten, the children participate in a program that balances academics and creative learning experiences. While the focus of our attention in first grade is on the academic program, we encourage the children to think critically and creatively. 'Hands-on' activities are provided throughout our program."

CHALLENGER. 5301 Curtis St., Fremont 94538. (510) 440-0424. Stella Dressler, Principal. Proprietary.

K-gr. 5, 450 students.(Plans to expand to gr. 6-8 in future.) K, half day, $3042; full day K & new gr. 1-5, $4932; returning gr. 1-5, $4617. Books: K, $50; gr. 1-5, $125. SDH: half day K, 8:40-11:40 or 12:30-3:30; all day K & gr. 1-8, 8:45-3:30. EDC: 7 am-6 pm, not open during school holidays. Uniforms. Afterschool dance, foreign language, karate, music, & art lessons. Admissions test. Waiting list. Summer program. Accredited by National Independent School Association.

"Since 1963, Challenger has been helping children grow into capable, happy, and responsible adults. Our four basic goals are to help children gain the bedrock of knowledge, learn to think logically and independently, become responsible for themselves, and discover the joy of learning. Challenger is well known for its high standards of academic excellence and student comportment."

LITTLE LEARNERS. 30540 Mission Blvd., Hayward 94544. (510) 471-6121. Marsha Campbell, Director. Est. 1973. Non-profit.

K-gr.2. $258/mo. Reg. fee $100. No fin. aid. SDH: K, 8:30-11:30 or 8:30-2; gr. 1-2, 8:30-2:30. EDC: 7 am-6 pm; $130/mo.; open during school holidays. Avg. class size 10, max. 12; classroom aides. Small facility with strong academic program, including computer literacy. Summer program from July 1 to mid. Aug. Students entering kdg. must be 4.5 yrs. by Sept. Parent participation encouraged, monthly parent meeting.

"The school is committed to individualized attention and learning that lays a firm foundation for a lifetime love of learning."

MONTESSORI CHILDREN'S SCHOOL. 1836 B St., Hayward 94541. (510) 537-8155. Susan C. Nolan, Director. Est. 1985. Non-profit.

Preschool-gr. 6; 70 students. $2200-$4250. Inc. fees $250. No fin. aid. SDH: K, 9-12 or 9-3; gr. 1-6, 9-3. EDC: 7:30 am-6 pm, $3/hr.; open on all but legal holidays. Avg. class size 18, max. 24. Teacher/student ratio 1:8. Individualized academics, bi-annual academic testing. Elem. instrumental music; computers; combined age levels; clean, visually stimulating, abundantly equipped classrooms; animals & garden. Summer program includes Montessori curriculum, outdoor games, motor skills development, art & dramatic play, science, cooking, Enrollment accepted year-round. Acceptance to kdg. based on readiness.

"Our program allows children to proceed at their own pace, promotes self-motivation and curiosity, and builds confidence and self-discipline. The program is one which promotes an atmosphere of respect for the child and his right to work without interruption at activities with a purpose."

MONTESSORI SCHOOL OF FREMONT. 155 Washington Blvd., Fremont 94539. (510) 490-0919. Tess Buenaventura, Director. Est. 1970. Proprietary.

2 yrs.-gr. 4; 75 students. $425-$445/mo. Inc. fees $175. No fin. aid. SDH: K, 8:45-2:45; gr. 1-4, 9-3. EDC: 7 am-8:45 ($30/mo), 2:45- 6 pm ($100/mo); $115 for am & pm; open on school holidays. Preschool-kdg. 48 students/4 teachers. Gr. 1-4, class size varies. Math specialist. Afterschool gymnastics, Aikido, piano keyboard, dance, computer Logo. Parents asked to help with gr. 1-4 field trips. Apply anytime. 10 wk. summer sports & academic camp. Parenting education available.

Our goal is "to assist the child to attain his/her maximum potential through a well-prepared environment supportive of the child's physical, spiritual, intellectual, and social needs. Well-prepared adults are ready to nurture and provide opportunities to guide children toward independence and responsibility."

NEW HORIZONS. 2550 Peralta Blvd., Fremont 94536. (510) 791-5683. FAX: (510) 791-9261. Kathryn Liu, Director. Marilyn Shaner, Admissions. Est. 1988. Proprietary.

Preschool-gr. 8; 100 students. $400/mo. Inc. fees $200. SDH: 8:30-3. EDC: 6:30 am-6:30 pm; fee included in tuition. Computer lab, library, math & science lab. Specialists teach music, art, Spanish, computers. On site specialist for children with learning differences. Afterschool dance, drama, chorus, & art. Continuous enrollment as long as space avail.; children accepted for kdg. if ready for program. Summer program in July & Aug. includes swimming & bowling. Accredited by Workshop Way Inc.

"We provide an excellent academic program, balanced with the arts. All reading & math is individualized for each child. We recognize learning differences with a multi-modality approach."

SEMORE. 4312 Dyer St., Union City 94587. (510) 471-1774. Mala Ahuja, Director. Est. 1968. Proprietary.

K-gr. 3; 47 students. $370/mo. Inc. fees $100. No fin. aid. SDH: 8:30-3. EDC: 6:30 am-6 pm; $28/mo; open on school holidays. Avg. class size 16-18, max. 20. Classroom aides. Extracurricular programs include music appreciation, computers, P.E., & Spanish. Afterschool "whiz kids" program. Active parents club. Summer programs. Apply at any time.

"Our excellent, trained and experienced staff provides children with a well organized and rich environment that enhances learning and growth."

WOODROE WOODS SCHOOL, INC. 22502 Woodroe Ave., Hayward 94541. (510) 582-3273. K-gr. 2; 60 students.

Dublin ◆ Pleasanton ◆ Livermore ◆ Sunol

CATHOLIC ELEMENTARY SCHOOLS

ST. MICHAEL'S. 372 Maple St., Livermore 94550. (510) 447-1888. Sister Emmanuel, O.P., Principal. Est. 1913. Non-profit.

K-gr. 8, 350 students. $1830-$2200. Reg. fee $150. 3% receive fin. aid. SDH: K, 8:15-11:25 or 11:35-2:50; gr. 1-8, 8:15-2:50. EDC: 7 am-6 p.m., $2.50/hr.; closed on school holidays. Avg. & max. class size 40, classroom aides. Uniforms. Enrichment classes, computer lab. Parents expected to donate service hours. Waiting list. Accredited by WASC.

"St. Michael's School is an extension of the teaching ministry of the Catholic Church. We believe parents are the prime educators of their children. As dedicated and knowledgeable Catholic educators, we hope to instill Christian values and a sense of community as well as to enable the students to achieve academic success."

ST. RAYMOND. 11555 Shannon Ave., Dublin 94568. (510) 828-4064. Sr. Marie Myers, Principal. Est. 1986. Non-profit.

K-gr. 8; 274 students. SDH: 8-2:40. EDC: 7 am-6 pm, closed on school holidays. Uniforms. Avg. class size 30, max. 35; classroom aides. PE & computers for K-gr. 8, art class K-gr. 5, Spanish gr. 6-8. Service hours required of parents. Apply Feb 1- March 15. Accredited by WASC.

St. Raymond "provides high quality Catholic education in cooperation with the administration, faculty & parents. The staff is dedicated to providing an environment in which the whole child can grow in knowledge, preparing for responsible adulthood."

NON-CATHOLIC RELIGIOUS SCHOOLS

ADVENTIST CHRISTIAN. 2828 Marina Ave., Livermore 94550. (510) 449-5857. Naomi Wooten, Director. Est. in the 1960s. Non-profit.

K-gr. 8; 18 students. $2025/yr. 10% receive fin. aid. SDH: K, 8-11:30; gr. 1-8, M-Th, 8-3, F, 8-12. No EDC. Dress code. Individualized programs, peer tutoring, gym, Bible classes. Parent participation encouraged.

"This church-operated school's purpose is to educate students in a balanced atmosphere of spiritual, physical, mental, and social standards. We strive to provide a quality education."

CHRISTIAN CHILDREN'S ACADEMY. 1135 Bluebell Dr., Livermore 94550. (510) 373-2872. K-gr. 8.

OUR SAVIOR LUTHERAN. 1040 Florence Rd., Livermore 94550. (510) 455-5437. Loren Miller, Principal. Est. 1973.

Preschool-gr. 8, 311 students. K, $1727; gr. 1-8, $2764. 3% receive fin. aid. EDC $2.25/hr. Avg. & max. class size 26. School is moving to a new site in fall of '95. Afterschool sports for gr. 5-8. Open reg. in Feb.

"Our goal is to care for, nurture, & discipline the students & families that come to us so they will grow to a personal relationship with God."

ST. PHILIP LUTHERAN. 8850 Davona Dr., Dublin 94568. (510) 829-3857. Bette Stark, Principal. Est. 1984. Non-profit.

Preschool-gr. 7, 186 students. K-gr. 5 full day, $2920; gr. 6-7, $3120. Inc. fees $220. 5% receive fin. aid. SDH: K, 8:30-11:30 or 8:30-3; gr. 1-7, 8:30-3. EDC: 7 am-6 pm, $2.60/hr., sibling discounts. Avg. class size 20, max. 25; aides when classes are large. Uniforms. Instrumental music lessons, Spanish for gr. 4-7, basketball league, annual track meet. Gymnasium. Applications processed throughout the year; waiting list.

"St. Philip Lutheran School provides excellence in academics in a Christian environment with small class size and a credentialed faculty who model Christian values and challenge students to reach their potential."

VALLEY CHRISTIAN ELEMENTARY. 7997 Vomac Rd., Dublin 94568. (510) 828-4850. Donna Taigen, Principal. Est. 1969. Non-profit.

K-gr. 6, 550 students. $3600, sibling discounts. Reg. fee $80; books $50-$100. Fin. aid avail. SDH: K, 9-3; gr. 1-6, 8:45-3. EDC: 7 am-6 pm; am-$5, pm-$6, am & pm, $8. Avg. class size 25. Dress code. Two levels of kdg: child must be 5 by 9/1 for 2nd level, by 12/1 for 1st level. Bible study & computer instruction in all grades; mixture of secular & Christian textbooks. T.E.C.H. class for students who have difficulty focusing: max. 12 students with teacher and aide; $100 extra/month.

"Valley Christian Elementary School seeks to serve those of all Christian backgrounds and desires a spirit which is truly transdenominational in its attitude and emphasis...Each child is considered to be a unique individual before God. The responsibility for his/her growth and care lies, first of all, in the home. V.C.E.S. wishes to aid the parent in this role. Christian teachers bring a positive reinforcement of home values and a Biblically-based view of life within the various subject areas."

SECULAR SCHOOLS

CARDEN WEST. 4444 Black Ave., Pleasanton 94566. (510) 846-7171. Michele Myers, Director. Judee Risso, Admissions. Non-profit.

Jr. K-gr. 6; 75 students. $3950-$4300. Inc. fees $385. No fin. aid. SDH: K-gr. 1, 9-2:15; gr. 2-6, 8:30-3. EDC: 7 am-6 pm; $3.50/hr. or $125/mo., open on school holidays. Avg. class size 15-20, max. 21. Aides in Jr. K & K. Dress code. Music, French. Two consultants trained by Mae Carden. Families contribute 20 hrs/yr. Summer enrichment camp. Individualized teaching but no "special ed."

We believe in "success for every child, every day! Individualized approach to each child based on needs and abilities. Positive reinforcement."

FOUNTAINHEAD MONTESSORI. 6901 York, Dublin. (at the crossroads of 680 & 580 in the San Ramon Valley) Mailing address: 115 Estastes Dr., Dublin 94568. (510) 820-1343. Sarah Zimmerman, Director. Est. 1972. Non-profit.

K-gr. 3. $540. Inc. fees $25. No fin. aid. SDH: K, 9-12 or 9-3; gr. 1-3, 9-3. EDC: 7 am-6 pm, open on school holidays. Avg. class size 15, max. 24; classroom aides. Afterschool keyboard, dance & computer. Summer programs.

The school's "elementary program builds upon the pre-school basics of order & independence. Here children widen social interactions and academic pursuits in a fascinating world of didactic materials."

HACIENDA—A HEADS UP! SCHOOL. 4671 Chabot Ave., Pleasanton 94588. (510) 463-2885. Joanne Camara, Director. Est. 1993. Proprietary.

Two multi-age classes 6-9 yrs. & 9-12 yrs. $660/mo. No fin. aid. Full day, 12 mon. program from 7 am-6 pm.; closed only on business holidays. Avg. & max. class size 24. Montessori curriculum along with the best from other theories. Computer for each child, field trips, foreign languages. Team of teachers with a variety of specialties. Parent involvement welcome.

"We offer an individualized, developmental approach, attending to the child's emotional, social and character development as well as cognitive and academic development. Children learn to manage and direct their own learning. New technologies are incorporated."

QUARY LANE SCHOOL. 3750 Boulder St., Pleasanton 94566. (510) 846-9400. Mrs. Rhonda Davis, Director. Proprietary.

Jr. K-gr. 4; 100 students. $500/mo. Inc. fees $320. No fin. aid. SDH: 8:30-3. EDC: 6:30 am-6:30 pm.; $150/mo.; open during school holidays. Avg. class size 16; max. 20. Spanish, physical education, music, science lab, computer lab, Fri. morning assemblies, holiday & end-of-the year musicals. Apply in the spring. 11 wk. summer camp.

"At our school, we create a learning environment which nurtures a child's natural creativity and provides a solid academic base to encourage further exploration. The statement, 'I CAN MAKE A DIFFERENCE' has been adopted as our guiding philosophy from all of us at the The Quarry Lane School."

VALLEY MONTESSORI. 460 N. Livermore Ave., Livermore 94550. (510) 455-8021. Mary Ellen Kordas, Director; Dee Ferro, Admissions. Est. 1976. Non-profit.

Toddler-gr. 8; 240 students. $4600. 3% receive fin. aid. SDH: K, 9-12 or 12:30-3:30; gr. 1-8, 9-3. EDC: 7:30 am-5:30 pm; $3/hr. Avg. class size 24, max. 28; 2 teachers/class. Specialists teach Spanish, science, PE & music. Afterschool music & Monart art program. Each school year culminates with an overnight, outdoor education trip for gr. 1-3 and a two night outdoor trip for older students. Parent participation welcome, especially for field trips and resources. Apply by Aug. 1st; waiting list. Summer programs. Accredited by A.M.S.

"The philosophy of the Valley Montessori community is the encouragement of the child's interests and curiosity, and the development of responsible, independent thinking that fosters positive self-esteem."

ALAMEDA COUNTY PRIVATE SECONDARY SCHOOLS

AMERICAN HERITAGE CHRISTIAN. See listing under Non-Catholic Religious Schools in Hayward.

ARROWSMITH ACADEMY. 2300 Bancroft Way, Berkeley 94704. (510) 540-0440. William Fletcher, Director. Est. 1979. Non-profit.

Gr. 7-12; 97 students. Gr. 7-8, $7200-$8200; gr. 9-12, $8200-$8700. Extra fees for trips. 10% receive fin. aid. Avg. class size 10-11; max. 16. Open campus. Strong E.S.L. program; 45-50% students of color. French & Spanish. 1 AP class. Students placed in classes according to ability level but no tracking. 90% of grads. attend 4 yr. college; 5% attend 2 yr. colleges. College counselor. SAT scores for '95 grads: V 521, M 524. Accredited by WASC.

Arrowsmith Academy provides a "multicultural, college prep program which develops young people with a diversity of teaching styles, small class sizes and a progressive point of view."

BEACON HIGH SCHOOL. 2000 Dennison St. Oakland 94606. (510) 436-6462. Thelma A. Farley, Director of Education; Aubyn Boyer, Admissions. Est. 1991. Non-profit.

Gr. 9-12, 80 students. $2620/trimester. $120 books & labs; $500 building fund. 10% receive fin. aid. Avg. class size 15, max. 20. Open campus. Ability grouping in academic classes. Spanish. College counselor. 80% of grads. go to 4 yr. colleges, 10% to 2 yr. SAT scores (75%): Class of '95, V 478, M 489; '94, V 463, M 512. Openings for each trimester in Sept., Jan. & April; monthly open houses.

"Beacon High School is a developmentally responsive, comprehensive high school emphasizing cooperative learning among students and collaborative relationships between students and teachers."

BISHOP O'DOWD HIGH SCHOOL. 9500 Stearns Ave., Oakland 94605. (510) 577-9100. Richard Ranaletti, Principal; Janet Vax, Admissions. Est. 1951. Non-profit.

Catholic, gr. 9-12; 1050 students. $5,250. Inc. fees $300. 10% receive fin. aid. Avg. class size 28; max. 35. Closed campus. Transportation avail. through AC Transit. French, German, Spanish; 11 AP classes. Extensive fine arts & athletic programs. Ability grouping in academic classes. College counselor. Summer school for remedial instruction. Applicants accepted according to scores on STS high school placement test, interview & previous school records. Waiting list. Accredited by WASC & WCEA.

89% of graduates go on to 4 yr. colleges; 10 % to two year colleges. SAT scores (99%): Class of '94, V 485; M 550; Class of '93, V 494, M 548.

"Bishop O'Dowd is a Catholic, coeducational, college prep high school which affirms the values of Christianity and the Catholic faith."

CHINESE CHRISTIAN. See listing under Non-Catholic Religious Schools in San Leandro.

CHRISTIAN HERITAGE ACADEMY. See listing under Non-Catholic Religious Schools in Fremont.

THE COLLEGE PREPARATORY SCHOOL. 6100 Broadway, Oakland 94618. (510) 652-0111. Dr. Janet Schwarz, Headmistress; Lucia H. Heldt, Admissions. Est. 1960. Non-profit.

Gr. 9-12; 318 students. $11,950. Inc. fees $500. 17% receive fin. aid. Avg. class size 16. Open campus. Bus service from some areas. Extensive programs in the arts (music, drama, visual arts), debate, community service and sports. German, Japanese, French, Spanish, Latin. College counselor. AP classes. Accelerated High school program at UCB. Apply by Jan. 19; waiting list. Admissions based on grades, teacher recommendations, entrance exam, interview and student's willingness to contribute to the lives of others. CPS recruits qualified students from a variety of cultural, economic, & ethnic backgrounds. Summer academic enrichment program for gr. 6-8. Accredited by WASC & CAIS.

100% of grads. go to 4 yr. colleges. SAT scores (100%): Class of '95, V 637, M 678; Class of '94, V 623, M, 655; Class of '93, V 617, M 654.

"CPS offers a rigorous academic program for young people who are potential candidates for four year colleges or universities. The school's *raison d'etre* is to provide this highly selective group of students with a program that will stimulate their intellectual curiosity and growth. At the same time, the school seeks to conduct its overall program in an atmosphere of mutual trust and friendliness, a climate conducive to the development of the highest human and moral values."

GOLDEN GATE ACADEMY. See listing under Non-Catholic Religious Schools in Oakland..

FREMONT CHRISTIAN. See listing under Non-Catholic Religious Schools in Fremont.

THE HEAD-ROYCE SCHOOL. See listing under Secular Schools in Oakland.

HOLY NAMES. 4660 Harbord Dr., Oakland 94618. (510) 450-1110. Sister Adele Hancock, Principal. Sister Anne Dinneen, Admissions. Est. 1868. Non-profit.

Catholic, girls; gr. 9-12, 310 students. $4500. Inc. fees $225. 20% receive fin. aid. Avg. class size 24, max. 30. Uniforms. Closed campus. Ability grouping in academic classes. AP English, French, Spanish & Art. Extensive Fine Arts Program, wide use of technology in all classes, broad-based Community Service Program. Midsession: 2 wks. of extra classes, travel, business or service internships. 87% of grads. go on to 4 yr. colleges; 12% to 2 yr. college counselor. 5 wk. academic summer program. Accredited by WASC & WCEA.

"HNHS provides a quality college preparatory education for young women in a supportive environment which fosters a Christian life view, which promotes academic excellence, and which values each individual in its culturally and ethnically diverse student body. HNHS prepares young women for entering and succeeding in higher education, for citizenship in our global and technological society, and for assuming expanding responsibilities as women and leaders of the 21st century."

KINGS ACADEMY. See listing under Non-Catholic Religious Schools in Newark.

LANDMARK BAPTIST. See listing under Non-Catholic Religious Schools in Hayward.

MAYBECK. 2362 Bancroft Way, Berkeley 94704. (510) 841-8489. Stanley Cardinet & Gretchen Griswold, Directors. Trevor Cralle & Mary Ann Brewin, Admissions. Est. 1972. Non-profit.

Gr. 9-12, 110 students. $6000. Inc. fees $500; books & field trips about $280/yr.. 15% receive fin. aid (max. 50% of tuition). Avg. class size 10, max. 18. Open campus. Campus near BART & buses. French, Spanish. Qualified students participate in accelerated program at UCB. Wk. long camping trip in Sept; 15 day special program in early spring allows students to choose from a variety of programs (i.e, community service, book design for authors & artists) and trips; 5 day end-of-the-year trip. College counselor. 85% of grads. attend 4 yr. colleges, 10% attend 2 yr. U.S. History offered in summer school.

"Maybeck works to achieve a union between the traditional study of academic subject matter and an innovative use of environment, through camping trips, international travel, community service and other special programs."

MOREAU CATHOLIC. 27170 Mission Blvd., Hayward (510) 881-4300; Admissions (510) 881-4320. Dr. Joseph Connell, President; Ms. Patricia Geistera, Principal; Scott T. Harrington, Admissions. Est. 1965. Non-profit.

Gr. 9-12; 1250 students. $4788. Reg. fee $285. 15% receive fin. aid. Closed campus. Avg. class size 32, max. 36. Dress code. Spanish, French, Latin, German. 14 AP classes; honors classes in English, mathematics, social studies & foreign languages. 4 full time counselors. 25 clubs and co-curriculars. Campus ministry program. 18 sports programs, 50 athletic teams. Apply by end of Jan., placement test in Feb; waiting list. Summer school. Accredited by WASC & WCEA.

College counselor. 65% of grads go to 4 yr. colleges, 30% to 2 yr. SAT's (85%): Class of '94, V 510, M 580; '93, V 510, M 570.

"Moreau Catholic High School affirms the traditions and values of Christianity and the Catholic faith while providing a college-preparatory curriculum. Moreau is a special community which strives to meet the life needs of the individual student."

PATTEN ACADEMY. See listing under Non-Catholic Religious Elementary Schools in Oakland. .

REDWOOD CHRISTIAN JUNIOR & SENIOR HIGH SCHOOL. 1500 Dayton Ave., San Leandro (510) 352-8330. See listing under Non-Catholic Religious Elementary Schools in Castro Valley .

SHADY GROVE SCHOOL. 17967 Almond Rd., Castro Valley 94546. (510) 537-3088. John Livergood, Director. Est. 1970. Non-profit.

Gr. 7-12; 10-20 students. $5200. Inc. fees $750. No fin. aid. In major curriculum areas, students are grouped according to academic and social maturity, interests and talents. Comprehensive, well-rounded education designed to develop in students a positive attitude toward learning. Spanish. Field trips integral part of the curriculum. Extended trips have included the Grand Canyon, Canada, Washington D.C. & Ashland Shakespeare Festival. Facilities include shop, studio, & swimming pool. Students also encouraged to take classes at the community college, adult schools, local seminars. Accredited by WASC.

"Shady Grove strives to provide a liberal yet rigorous approach to basic academic training. . .to create a school community which has a family orientation and focuses on individual responsibility and mutual respect. . . to personalize and individualize each student's learning program. . . to maintain a small student/teacher ratio. . .to respond immediately and intimately to students and parents . . . and to directly involve students in the planning and implementation of their learning process."

ST. ANDREW MISSIONARY BAPTIST. See listing under Non-Catholic Religious Schools in Oakland.

ST. ELIZABETH HIGH SCHOOL. 1530 34th Ave., Oakland 94601-3024. (510) 532-8947. Mathilda Ignacio, Principal; Ray Troper, Admissions. Est. 1921. Non-profit.

Catholic, gr. 9-12; 320 students. $4105. Inc. fees $250. 40% receive fin. aid. Closed campus. Avg. class size 28; max. 34. Transportation through Bart & AC transit. Uniforms. No ability grouping in academic classes. Spanish. College counselor. Placement tests given in Feb. & March. 60 % of grads. go to 4 yr. colleges; 38% to 2 yr. Accredited by WASC & WCEA.

"We believe education has the power to liberate; that all students should have access to Catholic education; that parents are primary educators; that teachers are facilitators of learning and that students are vested with dignity, worth, and value and are empowered by God to attain their potential and to contribute in a positive way to church and society."

ST. JOSEPH-NOTRE DAME HIGH SCHOOL. 1011 Chestnut St., Alameda 94501. (510) 523-1526. Anthony Aiello, Principal; Julie Thomas, Admissions. Est. 1881. Non-profit.

Catholic, gr. 9-12; 585 students. $4190. Inc. fees $290. 16% receive fin. aid. Closed campus. Avg. class size 25, max. 32. Computer lab, art studio, band room and science lab. French & Spanish. Honors classes, 3 AP classes. 96% of grads. attend 4 yr. colleges. 6 wk. summer school. Placement exam in early Feb. Accredited by WCEA & WASC.

"SJND acknowledges parents as the primary educators. We build upon Catholic values, provide quality instruction, foster a feeling of security and acceptance, and offer opportunities to join a caring community of faith and service. Diversity is valued and each student is made to feel a part of our community "

ST. MARY'S COLLEGE HIGH. Peralta Park, Berkeley 94706-2599. (510) 526-9242. Catholic, Boys, 400 students.

VALLEY CHRISTIAN JUNIOR/SENIOR HIGH. 10800 Dublin Blvd., Dublin 94568. (510) 828-4627. Donna Taigen, Principal. Ext. 1984. Non-profit.

Gr. 7-12, 284 students. Gr. 7-8, $4300; gr. 9-12, $5200. Sibling discounts. Inc. fees, $250-$300. Closed campus. Dress code. Avg. & max. class size 25. 49 acre campus with 25 classrooms, gym & athletic fields. Spanish, French, German & Japanese. 5 or 6 AP classes. All students complete 5 hrs. of community service/semester. Independent Study Program (ISGI) also offered, fee based on number of classes student takes. College counselor; 90% of grads. attend 4 yr. colleges. Accredited by WCEA & ACSI.

". . . The establishment and operation of Valley Christian High School is directed toward these goals: to effect an internalization of Christian principles as a way of life; to maintain academic excellence and intellectual growth; to live a disciplined life; to generate responsibilities for good citizenship; to train the body."

ALAMEDA COUNTY
SPECIAL EDUCATION SCHOOLS

BEACON DAY. See listing under Secular Elementary Schools in Oakland..

BEACON HIGH. See listing under Alameda County Secondary Schools.

BERKELEY ACADEMY. 2880 Sacramento 94702. (510) 848-4157. FAX: 848-2923. Charles Blakeney, Director. Est. 1979. Non-profit.

Girls, 12-18 yrs. $117/day. Referrals from county agencies and local school districts. Avg. class size 6, max. 12; teacher student ratio 1:4. Residential treatment, special education, day treatment and individual and family counseling for seriously emotionally disturbed and maltreated adolescent girls and their families.

"The girls for whom we provide direct service. . .have been assaultive and self-destructive; girls who run away and girls who hide in closets. They are diagnosed as schizophrenic and suicidal. They are overwhelmingly sexually abused, often physically, and severely neglected. At Berkeley Academy, we use a model of care, treatment and education which is based on principles of democracy and developmental psychology."

FRED FINCH YOUTH CENTER. 3800 Coolidge Ave., Oakland 94702. (510) 482-2244. James R. Williams, Director.

12-17 yrs; 50 students; boarding. 100% funded by public school. 5 hr. school day, operates year-round 235 days. Avg. class size 10, max. 12. 1 teacher: 6 students. The school serves seriously emotionally disturbed students and provides comprehensive mental health treatment program in a residential setting. Admissions accepted year-round. Certified by State Dept. of Education.

LINCOLN CHILD CENTER. 4368 Lincoln Ave., Oakland 94602. (510) 531-3111. Rachel Wylde, Director. Non-profit.

5 yrs.-16 yrs; 75 students. 100% funded by public school districts. SDH: 9-2:45. Extended school year, 11 month program. Avg. class size 9, max. 10. 1 teacher:3 students. The school serves students who are severely emotionally dis-

turbed, learning disabled, have attention deficit disorder or speech and language problems. It is associated with a residential and day treatment program and offers individual, family, and group therapy. Referrals, usually made by public school districts, county mental health services, or social services, accepted throughout the year.

"Lincoln Child Care provides a therapeutic, structured, and academically enriching setting that provides specialized treatment for the educational and emotional needs of children."

RASKOB DAY. 3520 Mountain Blvd., Oakland 94619. (510) 436-1275. John M. Davis, Ph.D., Director. Est. 1973. Non-profit.

Gr. 2-8; capacity for 36 students in 3 classrooms. $7560. Inc. fees $45. 5-10% funded by public school districts. 30% receive fin. aid. SDH: 8:30-2:30. Avg. class size 11, max. 12. Classroom aides. Comprehensive full-time program for students with learning disabilities or academic difficulties. The program focuses on serving students of average or above average potential who have not profited sufficiently from conventional classroom instruction. Teaching techniques & materials tailored to individual needs. The school is located on the campus of Holy Names College and students use college facilities for daily physical ed. program. Students attend weekly classroom problem solving sessions conducted by a counselor and have access to computer lab and library. Parent group aids in fund raising and field trips. On-going admissions; diagnostic evaluation required. Part-time remedial program year-round. Accredited by California Association of Private Specialized Education and Services. Certified by State Dept. of Ed.

Raskob has a "holistic orientation to the individual and stresses the importance of considering medical, psychological, academic and environmental issues in structuring a multisensory intervention program."

SENECA CENTER. 2275 Arlington Dr., San Leandro 94578. (510) 481-1222. Shirley Haberfeld, Director. Est. 1985. Non-profit.

6-16 yrs.; 96 students. 100% paid by public school funds. Students placed in school by the special ed. departments of their public school districts. Avg. class size 11-12, max 12; adult student ratio 1:4. SDH: 8:15-3. EDC: 3-5 pm. Transportation provided by school districts. Seneca serves the seriously emotionally disturbed with an intensive special education program and psychological, psychiatric and therapeutic services. Individual, family, and group counseling; speech pathologist, art therapist, & crisis intervention specialist. Highly structured behavioral program prepares students for smooth transition back to regular education. Residential Treatment also avail. 2nd campus in Fremont (226-6180). Certified by State Dept. of Ed.

Seneca provides "an outstanding and unconditional continuum of care for the most seriously troubled children and their families in Northern California."

SHADY GROVE SCHOOL. See listing under Alameda County Private Secondary Schools.

SPECTRUM CENTER. 879 Grant Ave., San Lorenzo 94580. (510) 278-6615.

Ages 5-22 yrs.; 60 students. 100% funded through public schools. Avg. class size 8, max. 10. Teacher/student ratio 1:3 (or smaller). Spectrum serves students with severe developmental disabilities and challenging behaviors when there is no appropriate public school placement. Positive behavior intervention case manager, speech pathologists, special education teachers. 6 wk. extended year summer school. Certified by Calif. Dept. of Education.

"Spectrum Center's philosophy is based on the belief that all individuals have a right to an education which promotes independence to the greatest degree. The school program addresses student needs in areas of independent living, community integration, recreation, leisure & vocational training."

STELLAR ACADEMY FOR DYSLEXICS. P.O. Box 7572, 4360 Hansen Ave., Fremont 94537-7572. (510) 713 -2471. Judy Gray, Principal; Barbara Gould, Admissions, Est. 1988. Non-profit.

Gr. 1-8; 28 students. $8914. No fin. aid. 10% of students supported by public school funds. SDH: 8:30-2:45. Avg. class size 10, max. 12; classroom aides. Stellar Academy offers educational services for Specific Language Disability, dyslexic children and their families using the Slingerland approach. Emphasis is placed on an optimal learning environment addressing the needs of the individual student. Parent participation welcomed. Applicants given Slingerland screening & WISC -R test. New students must attend summer school or receive min. of 10 hrs. of tutoring. Summer camp 6/26-7/21, 8:30-2:30; summer teacher training program 7/26-8/18, 9-noon. The school serves as a special education resource to the local community by conducting tutoring, workshops, referrals, and public outreach. Certified by State Dept. of Ed.

"The staff and board of Stellar Academy are dedicated to progressive, ongoing learning related to dealing with Specific Language Disability. We are committed to spreading the use of the Slingerland approach to classroom instruction and support national organizations whose goal is to educate the public about dyslexia."

VIA CENTER. 2126 6th St., Berkeley 94710. (510) 848-1616. Nicole Heare, Director. Est. 1988. Non-profit.

6-21 yrs.; 14 students. 100% funded by public districts. Avg. class size 7, max. 12. Teacher student ratio ranges from 1:1 to 1:3. SDH: 9:15-2:15. Extended year, 40 day summer program. Via provides an educational and therapeutic program for students with severe to moderate developmental disabilities who require intensive skills-building for a successful return to public school classrooms. Speech & Language Consultant and Behavior Analyst; transition services for students returning to regular classrooms; parent-staff training work-shops.   Certified by Calif. Dept. of Education.

Via's goal is "to help each student maximize his or her potential for happiness through independence by providing highly structured educational and behavioral programming within the context of a warm and family-like environment."

CONTRA COSTA COUNTY PRIVATE ELEMENTARY SCHOOLS

El Cerrito-Kensington-Richmond-San Pablo

CATHOLIC SCHOOLS

ST. CORNELIUS. 201 28th St., Richmond 94804. (510) 232-3326. Michael Mattos, Principal. Est. 1948. Non-profit.

K-gr. 8; 248 students. K, $285/mo; gr. 1-8, $235. Reg. fee $250. 5% receive fin. aid. SDH: 8:10-2:50. EDC: 6:45 am-6 pm; $2.65/hr.; closed during school holidays. Avg. class size 30, max. 35; 3 classroom aides. Gym & stage. Parents contribute 35 service units. Waiting list. Afterschool CYO sports. Accredited by WASC.

"St. Cornelius strives to encompass all facets of Christian living in its education of the whole child: spiritual, moral, intellectual, social, cultural, and physical."

ST. DAVID. 871 Sonoma St., Richmond 94805. (510) 232-2283. Barbara Berk Kringle, Principal. Est. 1963. Non-profit.

PreK-gr. 8; 336 students. $2170; sibling discounts. Reg. fee $200. 1% receive fin. aid. SDH: K, 8-11:30; gr. 1-8, 8-2:30. EDC: 6:30 am-6 pm; $3/hr. Closed on school holidays. Avg. class size 35, max. 36. Uniforms. Music, computers, foreign language, student government. Afterschool scouts & sports. Parents contribute 40 hrs./yr. Should apply by April but school accepts students until full. Accredited by WASC.

"We provide a Christian learning environment designed to develop a positive self-image where students can grow spiritually, intellectually, socially and physically."

ST. JEROME. 320 San Carlos Ave., El Cerrito 94530. (510) 525-9484; FAX: (510) 525-5227. Marla Korte, Principal. Est. 1955. Non-profit.

K-gr. 8; 304 students. $2500; 2 or more children, $4400. Reg. fee $260. Minimal fin. aid. SDH: K, 8:15-2:30; gr. 1-8, 8:15-2:55. EDC: 6:30 am-6:30

pm; $2.75/hr; closed on school holidays. Avg. class size 33, max. 36; aides in all grades. Uniforms. Instrumental music, dance, Spanish in gr. 7-8, library, student government. Afterschool sports for all grades. Counselor 2 days/wk. Single parents contribute 15 hrs/yr; two parent families contribute 30 hrs./yr. Apply in Jan., entrance test in early spring. Parents of prospective students encouraged to visit the school and classrooms and meet with the teachers. Waiting list for some grades. Accredited by WASC.

"St. Jerome Catholic School is dedicated to a Christian philosophy of education. We recognize that every person has equal dignity and an equal right to an education and we affirm the dignity and uniqueness of each child."

ST. JOHN THE BAPTIST. 11156 San Pablo Ave., El Cerrito 94530. (510) 234-2244. K-gr. 8, 315 students.

ST. PAUL. 1825 Church Lane, San Pablo 94806. (510) 233-3080. Ms. Sandra Colombo Hodges, Principal. Est. 1952. Non-profit.

K-gr. 8; 310 students. $2100 (parishioners)-$3450; sibling discounts. Reg. fee $200-$225. 5% receive fin. aid. SDH: K, 8-12 or 11-2:45; gr. 1-8, 8-2:45. EDC, closed on school holidays. Uniforms. Avg. & max. class size 35; aides in K-gr. 2. School social worker, Chapter One Program. Application period begins mid- Jan., remains open until grades are filled.; readiness test for kdg., placement test for other grades. Parents required to attend 4 meetings/yr. Afterschool CYO programs. Accredited by WASC.

"The philosophy of St. Paul School. . . is to impart through instruction and example, the truths of the Christian faith as found in the Roman Catholic tradition … to provide an academic curriculum and learning environment that enables students to achieve their learning potential and become responsible individuals in our Church and society… We celebrate the cultural diversity unique to our school, encouraging students to develop attitudes of mutual respect and understanding…"

NON-CATHOLIC RELIGIOUS SCHOOLS

ARLINGTON CHRISTIAN. 6382 Arlington Blvd., Richmond 94805. (510) 233-2556. J. Michael Callaghan, Director. Est. 1978. Non-profit.

K-gr. 12. $1800; reg fee $75. Sibling discounts. 10% receive fin. aid. SDH: 8:30-3. EDC: 6:30 am-6 pm; $2/hr.; open on school holidays. Avg. class size 22, max. 29-30. Uniforms. Accelerated Christian Education & School of Tomorrow Curriculum—individualized curriculum allows students to work at own level. Afterschool jr. high basketball. Child must be 4 by Sept. for kdg. Waiting list. Summer school for enrolled students. Accredited by A.C.E.

High School (gr. 7-12). Closed campus. Ability grouping in academic classes. Spanish, French, Greek. 75% of grads attend 4 yr. colleges.

"The primary objective of ACS is to train the student in the knowledge of God and the Christian way of life and to give the student an excellent education."

FAMILY CHRISTIAN. 160 Broadway, Richmond 94804. (510) 233-4827. Gr. 1-12, 18 students.

J.C. HAWKINS CHRISTIAN. 830 McDonald, Richmond 94801. (510) 233-8107. Wilma Hawkins, Principal. K-gr. 8, 50 students. Pentecostal.

TEHIYAH DAY. 2603 Tassajara Ave., El Cerrito 94530. (510) 233-3013. Dr. Revira Singer, Principal. Est. 1979. Non-profit.

K-gr. 8; 260 students. $6900-$7750. 32% receive fin. aid. SDH: K, 8:30-1:30; gr. 1-8, 8:30-3:30. EDC: until 6 pm; $4.25/hr.; closed on school holidays. School bus from No. Oakland & So. Berkeley; AC Transit # 7. Avg. class size 19, max. 24. Hebrew & Judaic Studies Program. Specialists teach art, computer, music, & library. Part-time LD specialist. Parents contribute 30 hrs./yr. Rolling admissions; waiting list. Must be 5 by Nov. 1 for kdg. 2 wk. Hebrew Ulpan in the summer. Accredited (provisionally) by CAIS.

"Tehiyah is a Jewish Community Day School committed to serving a diverse student body, maintaining academic excellence, and instilling in its students a love of learning, respect for individual differences, and a deep appreciation of Jewish values and culture."

VISTA CHRISTIAN SCHOOL. 2354 Andrade Ave., Richmond 94804. (510) 237-4981. Obadiah Patnaik, Principal; Mrs. Odling, Business Manager. Est. 1975. Non-profit.

K-gr. 8; 130 students. $230/mo. $50 application fee. Inc. fees: K-gr. 5, $115; gr. 6-8, $125. No fin. aid. SDH: 8:30-3. EDC: 7 am-6 pm; $100/mo.; closed on school holidays. Avg. class size 16; max. 20. Uniforms. A Beka Christian school curriculum. Tutoring available. Daily Bible classes in all grades. Active parent-teacher fellowship; room parents used; weekly chapel services with parents invited. All board members and personnel are born-again Christians in good standing with their churches. Stanford Achievement Test scores average 7 months above national average. Afterschool flag football, cheerleading, volleyball, basketball for gr. 6-8. 5 wk. full day summer school. Students admitted until classes are full. $15 testing fee for new students.

"Vista enrolls students without discrimination as to religion or race. We reserve the right to dismiss students unwilling to comply with school regulations or unable to achieve Vista's academic level."

SECULAR SCHOOLS

CANTERBURY. 312 D, Shane Dr., Richmond 94806. (510) 222-5050. Sharon Osteen, Director. Est. 1972. Proprietary.

K-gr. 8. $7380. No fin. aid. SDH: K, 9-2; gr. 1-8, 9-3:30. EDC: 7 am-6 pm; $2/hr. after 5 pm. Year-round school. Avg. class size 14, max. 18.

"Our goal is to provide an environment in which students are able to experience personal and academic success through guidance, instruction, and example."

EAST BAY SIERRA. 960 Avis Dr., El Cerrito, 94530. (510) 527-4714. Frederick W. Heinrich, Principal; Mary Lyman, Admissions. Est, 1983. Non-profit.

K-gr. 6; 310 students. $7500. Books & materials $235. 11% receive fin. aid. SDH: K, 8:30-1:30 (Sept.-Dec) 8:30-2:30 (Jan.-June); gr. 1-6, 8:30-3 (2:00 on Wed.). EDC: until 6 pm; $3.50/hr or $1250/yr; open on some school holidays. Avg. class size 22, max. 24. Aides in K-gr. 3; co-teachers in gr. 4-6. Bus from Montclair, Rockridge & South Berkeley. Specialists teach art, science, music, P.E., computers, French, Spanish. On-site L.D. specialist. Afterschool coed sports club & a wide variety of classes. Each family contributes min. of 10 hrs/yr. Apply by Dec. 15 for fall kdg; child must be 5 by Sept. 1. Accredited by CAIS/WASC.

"At Sierra, the acquisition of knowledge and skill goes hand in hand with the development of creative thinking, We believe that a child's success both in school and in later life is related to how much he or she enjoys the learning process and school. A fundamental goal at Sierra is to help our students develop a positive self-image, one that will enable them to approach academic challenges with courage, resourcefulness and confidence."

GOLDEN GATE APPLE. 379 Colusa, Kensington 94707. (510) 526-8570. K-gr. 12; 39 students.

THE PACIFIC ACADEMY OF NOMURA. 1615 Carlson Blvd., Richmond 94804. (510) 528-1727. Faith Nomura, Director. Est. 1964. Non-profit.

K-gr. 6; 140 students. $5750. Inc. fees $500. 6% receive fin. aid. SDH: 8:30-3. EDC: 7 am-6 pm; $3/hr.; open on school holidays. Avg. class size 16, max. 22; classroom aides. Uniforms. Music incorporated into every class on a daily basis. Curriculum geared towards hands-on experiences esp. in math, science, music & cultural studies. Japanese; music theory & performance; private piano, koto & violin lessons; computers, gymsters, art, chorus, Future Kids. Rascob Program for L.D. students. Open year-round. Summer program includes swimming. Parents contribute 10 hrs/student/yr. or $10 extra an hour,

"Music has a strong moral power. It fosters high levels of motivation in children and helps them learn the basics—reading, writing, and mathematics—more readily. Our program reflects a balance of arts, academics, and foreign language skills. The balance teaches our children about cooperation, participation, and appreciation; it enriches their lives."

PROSPECT. 2060 Tapscott Ave., El Cerrito 94530. (510) 232-4123. Dr. Leo Gaspardone, Director. Gail Berland, Admissions. Est. 1981. Non-profit.

K-gr. 6; 169 students. $7250. Inc. fees $150. 18% receive fin. aid. SDH: K, 8:45-2:20, gr. 1-6, 8:45-3. EDC: 2:20-5:30, sliding scale, closed on school holidays. Avg. class size 24, max. 25; classroom aides. Transportation avail. through private bus service. Extended study trips, strong drama program with school-wide productions. Specialists teach computers, art, Spanish, music, math lab, P.E., & movement. Afterschool soccer, tennis, basketball, ceramics, string music, chess, & piano. Parent participation encouraged under teacher supervision. Fall applicants should be tested & interviewed before March. For Kdg., child must be 5 by Sept 15. Summer enrichment programs in art, drama, travel. Beginning CAIS review.

"At Prospect School the nature and style of learning are as important as the product. We engage children in a process which emphasizes inquiry and conceptual learning. We want to teach children how to think as we present them with a curriculum worth thinking about."

WINDRUSH. 1800 Elm St., El Cerrito 94530. (510) 970-7580. Elizabeth Fox, Headmistress; Susan King, Admissions. Est. 1978. Non-profit.

K-gr. 8; 220 students. K-gr. 3, $6500; gr. 4-5, $6750; gr. 6-8, $7600. Fin. aid avail. SDH: K-gr. 3, 8:30-2:30; gr. 4-5, 8:30-3; gr. 6-8, 8-3. EDC: 7 am-6 pm; $1720/yr.; open on school holidays. Avg. class size 18, max. 22. 4 acre campus, full size gym, swimming program in fall & spring. Spanish taught K-gr. 8. Specialists teach art, music, computer, library; in mid. school, drama & martial arts. On-site L.D. specialist. Families contribute 20 hrs/yr; more involvement welcome. Afterschool middle school sports league. Applications accepted Nov. 1, acceptances sent out mid-March. Students must be working at grade level. Waiting list. 9 wk. summer camp. Accredited by CAIS & WASC.

Windrush is "built on a love of learning and accomplishment in a framework of academic excellence with a child-centered curriculum. The school has a commitment to diversity in its staff and student body and is a partnership among children, families, and staff."

El Sobrante ◆ Pinole ◆ Rodeo

CATHOLIC SCHOOLS

ST. JOSEPH. 1961 Plum St., Pinole 94564. (510) 724-0242. Kelly Stevens, Principal. Est. 1962. Non-profit.

K-gr. 8; 309 students. $2355. Inc. fees $160. SDH: K, 8:15-12; gr. 1-8, 8:15-3. EDC: 7 am-6:30 pm; $2.50/hr; closed on school holidays. Avg. class size 35, max. 36. Uniforms. CYO sports, yearbook, videography. Afterschool basketball & volleyball. Parents must contribute 30 hrs./yr. Apply by Dec. 15 for following year. Waiting list. Accredited by WASC.

ST. PATRICK. 907- 7th St., Rodeo 94572. (510) 799-2506. Sister Miriam Claire, Principal. Est. 1957. Non-profit.

K-gr. 8. Sibling discounts. SDH: 8:10-3. EDC: 7 am-6:30 pm; $3.50, cheaper rates by contract; closed on school holidays. Avg. class size 32, max. 34; aides in K & gr. 1. Uniforms. Spanish starting in gr. 4; computers starting in kdg; pre-Algebra in gr. 6; computer & science labs. On site L.D. specialist. Afterschool CYO boys basketball for gr. 5-8. Parents contribute min. of 20 hrs./yr. Inquire in Feb. for fall admission. Waiting list. Accredited by WASC.

"St. Patrick's is an academically oriented school, with its primary focus on educational basics, including, but not limited to fundamentals in elementary subjects, home study, parent involvement, and student responsibility. Advanced academics are taught in gr. 7 & 8. Religion is a graded subject."

NON-CATHOLIC RELIGIOUS SCHOOLS

BETHEL CHRISTIAN ACADEMY. 431 Rincon Ln., El Sobrante 94803. (510) 223-9550. K-gr. 8, 186 students.

CALVARY CHRISTIAN ACADEMY. 4892 San Pablo Dam Rd., El Sobrante 94803. (510) 222-1700. Preschool-gr. 12.

EL SOBRANTE CHRISTIAN. 5100 Argyle Rd., El Sobrante 94803. (510) 223-2242. C. Scott Wells, Principal. Est. 1971. Non-profit.

K-gr. 8, 410 students. K-gr. 5, $2310; gr. 6-8, $2500. Reg. fee $125, sports $25. No fin. aid. SDH: K-gr. 5, 8:45-3; gr. 6-8, 8:30-3. EDC: 7 am-6 pm, $2/hr., closed on school holidays. Avg. class size 22, max. 24. Dress code. Computer lab & library. Apply anytime; students must be at grade level. Must be 5 by 9/1 for kdg. Waiting list for some grades. Afterschool flag football, volleyball, basketball, softball, track for jr. high. Remedial & enrichment summer programs.

"ESCS seeks to educate students using the Bible as the core of our curriculum. Staff members are the 'living curriculum,' modeling Biblical principles in action."

SHERWOOD FOREST CHRISTIAN. 5570 Olinda Rd., El Sobrante 94803. (510) 223-6079. Craig Shaw, Principal. Baptist. K-gr. 8; 120 students.

Danville ◆ Lafayette ◆ Moraga ◆ Walnut Creek

CATHOLIC SCHOOLS

ST. ISADORE. 435 La Gonda Way, Danville 94526. (510) 837-2977. Kathy Gannon-Briggs, Principal. Est. 1962. Non-profit.

K-gr. 8; 384 students. $2670, sibling discounts. Reg. fee $150. SDH: K, 8-11 or 11:50-2:50; gr. 1-8, 8-2:50. EDC: 3-6 pm, sliding fee, closed on school holidays. Avg. class size 38, max. 40; full-time classroom aides. Uniforms. Art, dance, Spanish, computers, P.E. On-site L.D. specialist. Afterschool CYO sports. Blue Ribbon School. Waiting list. Accredited by WASC.

We "work towards the goal of every student being a successful learner in a Christ-centered environment."

ST. MARY. 1158 Bont Ln., Walnut Creek 94596. (510) 935-5054. Barbara McCullough, Principal. Est. 1960. Non-profit.

K-gr. 8, 295 students. $2830. Reg. fee $150. 3% receive fin. aid. SDH: K, 8:10-12 (3 days/wk) 8:10-2:50 (2 days); gr. 1-8, 8:10-2:50. EDC: $3/hr., closed on school vacations. Max. class size 34; classroom aides. Uniforms. Art enrichment, community outreach. Resource specialist on site 2 days/wk. for L.D. students. Specialists teach Spanish & computers. Afterschool basketball, volleyball, scouts. Parents contribute 40 hrs./yr. Accredited by WASC.

"We believe that our responsibility is to work in partnership with parents to provide a nurturing Christian environment in which we offer an enriched academic program to encourage the love of learning. We foster a sense of self-worth and dignity in each individual and an acceptance of others as reflecting Christ. We prepare students to be Christian witnesses by putting faith into action."

ST. PERPETUA. 3445 Hamlin Rd., Lafayette 94549 (510) 284 1640. Linda R. Story, Principal. Est. 1963. Non-profit.

K-gr. 8, 283 students. In parish, $2550; out of parish $2950. Sibling discounts. Inc. fees $200. Fin. aid avail. SDH: K, 8-12; gr. 1-8, 8-2:40. EDC: 7 am-6 pm; $2.50/hr. on reg. basis; $3/hr. drop-in; sibling discounts; closed on school holidays. Uniforms. Avg. class size 31, max. 35; classroom aides in K-gr. 5. Music, dance computer, Spanish in upper grades. Families contribute 35 hrs./yr. Afterschool CYO basketball, track, volleyball. Apply by April 1. Accredited by WASC.

"St. Perpetua is a Catholic parish school where parents and staff work together to develop the God given potential of each child. This environment, based on Christian values, supports a faith community in which responsibility, independence, leadership, and academic growth are promoted."

NON-CATHOLIC RELIGIOUS SCHOOLS

SAN RAMON VALLEY CHRISTIAN ACADEMY. 220 W. El Pintado Rd., Danville 94526. (510) 838-9622. Christina Johnson, Principal. Est. 1979. Non-profit.

K-gr. 8; 220 students. K-gr. 6, $3363; gr. 7-8, $3477. 6% receive fin. aid. SDH: K, 8:30-11:25 or 12:05-3; gr. 1-6, 8:30-3; gr. 7-8, 8:10-3. EDC: 11:30 am-6 pm, closed on school holidays. Dress code. Avg. class size: K-gr. 6, 26; gr. 7-8, 22. Max. class size 26. Library, science & computer labs, gym, Spanish for all grades, hot lunch program, electives for gr. 7-8. 3 day outdoor ed. for gr. 5 & 6; Wash. D.C. trip for gr. 7 & 8; 8th grade play. Speech meet, band, choir. Parent participation required in school service program. Applications accepted in Sept. for following year; priority to siblings and CPC Church members; child must be 5 by Oct. 1 for kdg; waiting list in some grades. Afterschool athletics for gr. 6-8. Summer computer & art programs. Accredited by WASC & ACSI.

"SRVA exists to serve Jesus Christ and through the perspective of His word and endeavors to meet the students' spiritual, academic, social, and physical needs."

TRINITY LUTHERAN. 2317 Buena Vista Ave., Walnut Creek 94596. (510) 935-3362. (510) 935-3362. Linda Duesler, Principal. Est. 1981. Non-profit.

PreK-gr. 5. $2800. Inc. fees $205. 2% receive fin. aid. SDH: K, 8:30-12:30; gr. 1-5, 8:30-3. EDC: $2.50-$3/hr.; open on school holidays. Uniforms. Avg. class size 15, max. 24; classroom aides. Choral music, Spanish, nondenominational religion. Parents contribute 20 hrs. per yr. per child. 10 wk. summer program.

Trinity Lutheran School provides a "loving, caring environment with credentialed and dedicated staff. It is a small school that provides an academically and artistically rich program and works on building the child's self-esteem and sense of community. "

WALNUT CREEK CHRISTIAN ACADEMY. 2336 Buena Vista Ave., Walnut Creek 94596. (510)935-1587. K-gr. 8, 300 students.

WOODLANDS CHRISTIAN. 2721 Larkey Ln., Walnut Creek 94596. (510) 945-6863. N. Edmiston, Principal. Est. 1981. Non-profit.

PreK-gr. 8; 285 students. (Contra Costa Christian High School at same location; see listing under Contra Costa County Private Secondary Schools.) $2508-$4080. Enr. fee $200. Fin. aid avail. SDH: 8-2:40. EDC: $3.25/hr., open on school holidays. Avg. class size 23, max. 25. Dress code. Music, computers, foreign language. Afterschool sports, Spanish & gymnastics for gr. 6-8. Resource room assistance provided for students with learning differences. Parents must be Christian & attend church. Waiting list. Accredited by WASC.

"Walnut Creek Christian Schools subscribe to a Christian philosophy of education based on God's truth as revealed in the Bible. We are dedicated to developing from a Christian perspective our students' endowments for knowing, choosing, and for acting."

SECULAR SCHOOLS

THE DORRIS-EATON SCHOOL. 1847 Newell Ave., Walnut Creek 94595. (510) 933-5225. Gerald Ludden, Director. Est. 1954

Preschool-gr. 8; 400 students. K-gr. 5, $7490; gr. 6-8, $7690. Evaluation fee $150. 5% receive fin. aid. SDH: 8:15-3. EDC: 7 am-6 pm; $1200/ yr; open on school holidays. Avg. class size 18, max. 22. Two classes for each grade Uniforms. Specialists teach Spanish, art, P.E., music, computer science. Afterschool sports, student council, & yearbook for gr. 6-8. Summer camps and academic program. Apply by March 1st. Entrance evaluations required of all new students.

"Dorris-Eaton is a private, independent, coeducational college-preparatory day school for preschool through junior high students. In small, moderately structured classrooms, where politeness and consideration are the norm, students engage in learning activities in a focused manner. Critical and creative thinking as well as organizational & study skills are taught at every grade level."

THE MEHER SCHOOLS. 999 Leland Dr., Lafayette 94549. (510) 938-4826. Ellen Evans, Director. Est. 1975. Non-profit.

PreK-gr. 5, 210 students. $2700 ('94-'95). No fin. aid. SDH: K, 8:35-2; gr. 1-5, 8:25-2:30. EDC: 7 am-6:30 pm, open on school vacations. Avg. class size 28 (w/2 teachers), max. 35. Classroom aides. Drama program, excellent library, art studio, small theater. Specialists teach art, theater & library skills. On site tutor for students with learning differences. Afterschool enrichment program, children's choir, art, woodshop, sports. Summer programs. Accredited by WASC.

The school's goal is "to prepare children fully to succeed in any educational environment while supporting individual abilities."

SAKLAN VALLEY. 1678 School St. Moraga 94556. (510) 376-7900 Patricia Corlett, Director; Mary Handler, Admissions. Est. 1978. Non-profit.

PreK-gr.8; 135 students. $5200-$6300. Mat. fees $300, testing $75, application fee $50. 15% receive fin. aid. SDH: K, 8:30-2; gr. 1-8, 8:30-3. EDC: 7 am-6:30 pm, $280/mo. or $3.50/hr.; open on school holidays. Avg. class size 14, max. 16; aides in kdg. Uniforms. Transportation to and from Lafayette & Orinda. Specialists teach music, French, Spanish, P.E., computers. Afterschool enrichment classes include instrumental music. Entrance testing in Feb. Waiting list. Summer day camp. Accredited by WASC, member of CAIS.

"SVS is dedicated to excellence in education. The purpose of the school is to assist in the development of well-adjusted, happy children who will acquire a sound academic foundation, an enthusiasm for learning, and a confident approach to life. The school's objectives are to encourage student curiosity and creativity, to develop critical thinking, problem solving and communication skills, and to stimulate awareness of the environment. The school promotes cooperative learning and thoughtfulness to others through responsible and ethical behavior."

THE SEVEN HILLS SCHOOL. 975 N. San Carlos Dr., Walnut Creek 94598. (510) 933-0666. FAX: (510) 933-6271. Bill Miller, Headmaster. Sue VanLandingham, Admissions. Est. 1962. Non-profit.

PreSchool-gr. 8; 295 students. $5217-$8828. 10% receive fin. aid. SDH: K-gr. 2, 8:15-2:30; gr. 3-8, 8:15-3. EDC: 6:30 am-6:30 pm; $735-$3125; open on school holidays. Uniforms. Avg. class size 13-16, max. 18. Aides in kdg. School bus picks up children in some areas. 9.5 acre campus, swimming pool, tennis courts, gymnasium. Hands-on, integrated curriculum. Specialists teach foreign languages, art, music, computers, library, & P.E. Afterschool sports for middle school students. Apply by Feb. 15; waiting list. Accredited by CAIS.

Concord ◆ Martinez ◆ Pleasant Hill

CATHOLIC SCHOOLS

CHRIST THE KING. 195 Brandon Rd., Pleasant Hill 94523. (510) 685-1109. Sister Timothy Anne, Principal. Est. 1961. Non-profit.

K-gr. 8; 340 students. $1940-$3580. Inc. fees $150. 3% receive fin. aid. SDH: Kdg., 3 hrs. am or pm; gr. 1-8, 8:20-2:45. EDC: 7 am-6 pm; $2.75/hr.; closed on school holidays. Avg. class size 35-40; max. 40. Aides in some classes. Uniforms. CYO Sports, student leadership, science fair, DARE. Afterschool sports, brownies, scouts. Parents contribute 30 hrs. of work/yr. to the school. Apply in Feb. for Sept. Kdg.; in April for other grades. Accredited by WASC.

"We are here to assist the parents in the religious education of their children. We teach all the other subjects that are taught in the public schools. We try to provide an excellent education for the children who attend Christ the King."

QUEEN OF ALL SAINTS. 2391 Grant St., Concord 94520. (510) 685-8700. Maureen Tiffany, Principal. Est. 1948. Non-profit.

K-gr. 8. $2353-$5981. 10% receive fin. aid. Inc. fees $300. SDH: 8:10-2:35. EDC: 7 am-6 pm, closed on school holidays. Avg. & max. class size 36, classroom aides. Uniforms. Parents contribute 40 hrs./yr. Afterschool basketball & track. Accredited by WASC.

"As Catholic educators we. . . offer a learning program that helps students grow in their own faith. . . Students are provided a basic academic foundation and challenged to expand their knowledge. . .We foster an appreciation of the special cultural heritage each child brings to enrich our school community. . .We strongly support responsible involvement in community service which incorporates faith, academics, and cultural gifts."

ST. AGNES. 3886 Chestnut Ave., Concord 94519. (510) 672-5862. Karen Mangini, Principal. Est. 1967. Non-profit.

K-gr. 8; 352 students. $2100. Inc. fees $150. SDH: 7:55-2:35. EDC: 7 am-6 pm; closed on school holidays.   Avg. class size 38, max. 40. Classroom aides. Uniforms. Computer lab, school counselors, Spanish for all grades, P.E. teacher, reading specialist. Parents contribute a minimum of 35 hrs./yr. Children must be 4 yrs., 10 mon. when kdg. starts. Afterschool track & basketball for boys & girls. Students score in 80 percentile on standardized tests. Accredited by WASC.

"At St. Agnes children come to grow, learn to care and leave to serve. We have creative, caring teachers, very supportive parents and cooperative, gentle children."

ST. CATHERINE OF SIENA. 604 Melius St., Martinez 94553. (510) 228-4140.

ST. FRANCIS OF ASSISI. 866 Oak Grove Rd., Concord 94518. (510) 682-5414. Sister Theodore Blake, Principal. Ann Bywater, Admissions. Est. 1965. Non-profit.

K-gr. 8, 350 students. $2460-$6110. Reg. fee $155. No fin. aid the 1st year. SDH: K, 8-11:15 or 10:15-1:30; gr. 1-8, 8-2:45. EDC: 6:45 am-6 pm, $3/hr. Avg. class size 38, max. 40; aides half day. Uniforms. Spanish & computer programs. Reading specialist. Parents contribute 30 hrs./yr. Call in Jan. for fall placement, testing March-April; waiting list.   Afterschool CYO sports. Accredited by WASC.

We are "committed to teaching skills and values needed to help our students live good Christian lives."

NON-CATHOLIC RELIGIOUS SCHOOLS

AGAPE CHRISTIAN. 444 Fig Tree Lane, Martinez 94553. (510) 228-8155. K-gr. 3, 45 students.

CHRISTIAN LIFE ELEMENTARY. 3950 Clayton Rd., Concord 94518. (510) 676-6422. K-gr. 6.

FIRST LUTHERAN. 4002 Concord Blvd., Concord 94519. (510) 671-9717. Lois Rosenberg, Principal; Jill Pitzlin, Admissions. Est. 1990. Non-profit.

K-gr. 5. $2550. Inc. fees $230. 10% receive fin. aid. SDH: 8:30-3. EDC: 7 am-6 pm; $2.25/hr; open on school holidays. Avg. class size 13, max. 25. Classroom aides. Relaxed dress code. Spanish in gr. 2-5, music program, computers in all classrooms, gymnasium. Modern, up-dated curriculum, phonetics. Tutoring avail. for students with mild learning disabilities. Active Parent-Teacher League, parent participation welcome. Afterschool Kids'Klub & Brownies. Open enrollment starts Feb. 1. 10 wk. summer program. Accredited by LCMS.

"Our staff exhibits a love of children and a concern for their spiritual and temporal well-being. They exemplify a living relationship with Jesus Christ and are dedicated to teaching as a ministry with high professional standards."

KING'S VALLEY CHRISTIAN. 4255 Clayton Rd., Concord 94521. (510) 687-2020. K-gr. 8, 340 students.

PLEASANT HILL JUNIOR ACADEMY. 796 Grayson Rd., Pleasant Hill 94523. (510) 934-9261. Denise White, Director. Est. 1953. Non-profit.

K-gr. 10. K, $1580-$2030; gr. 1-10, $1950- $3740. Higher fees for families that do not belong to a Seventh Day Adventist Church. Sibling discounts. SDH: K, 8:25-12; gr. 1-10, 8:25-3:15. EDC: 7 am-6 pm, $1.50/hr. Dress code.

YGNACIO VALLEY CHRISTIAN. 4977 Concord Blvd., Concord 94521. (510) 798-3131. Dan L. Shedd, Director. Est. 1972. Non-profit.

K-gr. 8, 186 students. $2600. Application fee $150. SDH: 8:40-3. EDC: 7 am-6 pm;$2.50/hr.; closed on school holidays. Avg. class size 20-24, max. 24; classroom aides. Dress code. Band, hand bell choir, computer class. Enroll March-Aug., Christian families only; waiting list in some grades. Afterschool intermural sports.

The school educates "for Christian leadership and character development" while providing "excellence in academics."

SECULAR SCHOOLS

BIANCHI ELEMENTARY. 4347 Cowell Rd., Concord 94518. (510) 680-8606. Sharon G. Passow, Principal. Est. 1974. Proprietary.

K-gr. 6, 80 students. $364-$575/mo. Books & reg. fee extra. No fin. aid. SDH: 8:30-3. Avg. class size 18, max. 22. Dress code. Specialists teach computer, art, music, enrichment. Summer programs.

Bianchi offers a "traditional, back-to-basics" program.

CONCORDIA. 2353 Fifth Ave., Concord 94518. (510) 689-6910. Jody Kresge, Director. Est. 1973. Proprietary.

PreK-gr. 6, 125 students. $235-$685/mo. Inc. fees $160. 15% receive fin. aid. SDH: 8:30-3. EDC: 6:30 am-6:30 pm, included in tuition. Dress code. Avg. class size 24, max. 30; 2-3 aides per class. Specialists teach P.E., art, music (concert recorders & chorus), Spanish, drama, computers. On site L.D. specialist. Developmentally based classes at all levels; Montessori learning activities; hands-on learning materials to teach concepts; caring teachers who foster values. Children accepted to kdg. if ready. Waiting list. Afterschool programs in "family-like" atmosphere emphasize arts, sports, and nature studies. Summer academic program and day camp. Accredited by Professional Association of Childhood Educators & American Montessori Society.

"The Concordia School is an academic community formed by parents, teachers and students. Our curriculum challenges students to use their intellectual and social skills and integrates the arts and sciences. . .We believe that the student who learns how to learn knows how to live. Thus, we offer the child a love of learning and foster the confidence for success in the years to come."

PATCHIN'S SCHOOLS. 1124 Ferry St., Martinez 94553-1721. (510) 228-1295. Richard & Barbara Patchin, Directors. Est. 1960. Proprietary.

Preschool-gr. 6. $375/mo. Reg. fee $25. No fin. aid. SDH: K, 8-2; gr. 1-6, 8-3. EDC: 6 am-6 pm. Avg. class size 12, max. 15. Dress code. Music, foreign languages, holiday and end-of-year programs, community outreach programs. Active parents' association. Afterschool arts & crafts, clubs, organized games. Apply year-round. Child must be 4 1/2 yrs. for kdg. Summer day camp and academic summer school.

Patchin's provides a "very individualized learning environment where children progress at the rate they are able to understand the concepts presented. Every effort is made to provide each student with a good, firm academic foundation for future learning and growth."

Antioch ◆ Brentwood ◆ Pittsburg

CATHOLIC SCHOOLS

HOLY ROSARY. 25 East 15th St., Antioch 94509. (510) 757-1270. Patricia McBride, Principal. Est. 1954. Non-profit.

Pre K-gr. 8; 350 students. $2100; sibling discounts. Reg. fee $125. 8% receive fin. aid. SDH: K, 8:15-11:15 & 12-3; gr. 1-8, 8:15-3. EDC: 6:30 am-6 pm. Avg. & max. class size 30; aides in K-gr. 2. Uniforms. Afterschool extracurricular activities. Waiting list. Accredited by WASC.

"HRS strives to meet the needs of the whole child in a challenging world."

ST. PETER MARTYR. 425 W. 4th St., Pittsburg 94565. (510) 439-1014. Joseph Siino, Principal. Est. 1950. Non-profit.

PreK-gr. 8; 285 students. $2520; sibling discounts. Reg. fee $225. 10% receive fin. aid. Avg. class size 30, max. 35. SDH: K, 8:15-11:30; gr. 1-8, 8:15-2:45. EDC: 7 am-5:30 pm, $2/hr, closed on school holidays. Uniforms. Computer lab, library, extended outdoor education programs. Chapter 1 program. Parent participation required. Afterschool sports, cheerleading squads, clubs, drama, computer, reading club, & student govt. Accredited by WASC.

"St. Peter Martyr School works with parents, who are the primary educators. Prime concern is with the total individual, including his/her religious, academic, emotional, social, physical, & cultural dimensions. The school is committed to share Christ's gospel through education."

NON-CATHOLIC RELIGIOUS SCHOOLS

ANTIOCH CHRISTIAN. 405 W. 6th St., Antioch 94509. (510) 778-1639. Larry L. Roper, Principal; Beverly Gono, Admissions. Est. 1986. Non-profit.

K-gr. 6. $1960. Inc. fees $175. 5% receive fin. aid. SDH: 8:30-3:15. EDC: 6 am-6 pm; $1.50/hr. Avg. class size 18, max. 21; one classroom aide. Uniforms. A-Beka curriculum. Gymnastics. Member of ACSI.

The school offers "academic excellence in a Christian environment."

ANTIOCH CHRISTIAN TUTORIAL. 640 E. Tregallas, Antioch 94509. (510) 757-1837. Pastor Hanford, Director. Est. 1986. Non-profit.

K-gr. 12, 100 students. $2200. Inc. fees $477. No scholarships. SDH: 8:30-2:45. Uniforms. Avg. class size 15, max. 25; classroom aides. Music, P.E., field trips, crafts. Special help available for students with learning differences. Students accepted year-round. Summer programs. Accredited by School of Tomorow.

High school program: Spanish, drama, music, college prep curriculum, 2 A.P. classes, computers, individualized program. College counselor. 80% of grads. attend 4 yr. colleges, 15% attend 2 yr. colleges.

"A.C.T.S. prepares leaders for life in Christian character and academics, making each person the best they can be in our ever changing world."

HERITAGE BAPTIST ACADEMY. 5200 Sand Creek Rd., Antioch 94509. (510) 778-2234. Dr. J. Mincey, Principal. Est. 1982. Non-profit.

K-gr. 12; 70 students. K-gr. 8, $2210; gr. 9-12, $2320. Reg. fee $125, books $150. No fin. aid. SDH: 8:30-3:30. EDC: 7 am-6 pm, $.75/15 min., closed on school holidays. Avg. class size 16, max. 22. Uniforms. New 10 acre campus. Band, computer. Gr. 9-12: Spanish, college counselor, 85% of grads. go to 4 yr. colleges, 10% to 2 yr. Parent participation encouraged. Summer day care and academics.

We "provide a thoroughly Christian atmosphere in order to provide high quality academic training with the ultimate goal of conforming students to the image of Jesus Christ."

HILLTOP SEVENTH DAY ADVENTIST CHRISTIAN. 320 Worrell Rd., Antioch 94509. (510) 778-0214. Monica R. Greene, Principal. Est. 1940's. Non-profit.

K-gr. 10, 106 students. Non-SDA's: K, $130/mo; gr. 1-8, $227.50/mo; gr. 9-10, $260/mo. Reg. fee $225. 25% receive fin. aid. SDH: K, 8:15-12, gr. 1-10, 8:15-3, 8:15-2 (Fri.). EDC: 3:15-5:30, $2.50/hr.; closed on school holidays. Avg. class size 15, max. 30; classroom aides. Dress code. Gymnasium, Spanish, outdoor education gr. 1-10. Students accepted regardless of family's religious beliefs. Waiting list in some grades. Summer enrichment & remedial programs. Accredited by Northern California Conference of Seventh Day Adventists.

SHORE ACRES CHRISTIAN. 500 Pacifica Ave., Pittsburg (Bay Point) 94565. (510) 458-2838. Marvin Brentley, Principal. Est. 1979. Non-profit.

K-gr. 12, 75 students. $1850. Books $200-$260. No fin. aid. SDH: M-Th, 8:30-3; Fri., 8:30-1:30. EDC: 6:30 am-6:30 p.m., $2/hr.; open on school holidays. Uniforms. Avg. class size 10, max. 15, classroom aides. Computers in all classrooms, P.E., library, art, Christmas program, poetry & literature gr. 7-12. Spanish for older students. A Beka and Bob Jones curriculum used. Parents must help with fundraisers. Afterschool activities vary. Apply anytime.

"Above everything else, we are ministers of the Gospel of Jesus Christ. Our desire is to promote academic and physical growth, but, most of all, spiritual maturity and a personal relationship with our Lord and Saviour."

SECULAR SCHOOLS

GREAT BEGINNINGS LEARNING CENTER. 512 Texas St., Antioch 94509. (510) 778-5462. Celeste Argel, Director. Est. 1988. Proprietary.

K-gr. 4, 45 students. $230/mo. Inc. fees $185. 5% receive fin. aid. SDH: 8:30-2:30. EDC: 6:30 am-6 pm; $130/mo; open on school vacations. Avg. class size 12, max. 15; aide helps with reading. Computers, library, instrumental music beginning in kdg. Afterschool sports coordinator. Applications accepted until classes are full. Program runs through summer months.

"Our basic premise is that each child should be treated and respected as an individual. Children are encouraged to develop to the height of their ability, through the guidance of creative teachers and interested parents."

WILLOW WOOD SCHOOL (AT DAINTY CENTER). 1265 Dainty Ave., Brentwood 94513. (510) 634-4539. Shawn & Adrienne Guinn, Directors. Martha Morado, Admissions. Est. 1980. Non-profit.

2 yrs-4th grade, 300 students. Tuition varies; 5% receive fin. aid. Avg. class size 12-20; max, K, 18, gr. 1-4, 20. SDH: K, 8:15-12:15; gr. 1-2, 8:15-2:30; gr. 3-4, 8:15-3. EDC: 6 am-6 pm, open on school holidays. National model & training program for "Tribes" self-esteem program; "Math Their Way" Program; "Right From the Start" reading; P.E.; arts & crafts. Two and a half acre facility includes an extensive farm which provides hands-on learning within a thematical, integrated curriculum: animal petting zoo, Delta pond, greenhouse, kids' planting area. Afterschool "Odyssey of the Mind" program. Extended family structure encourages high parent involvement. Year-round enrollment. Child must be 4 yrs., 8 months for kdg. Summer program includes swimming, bowling, biking, field-trips, drama, crafts.

"The primary goal we have is to allow kids to develop positive attitudes about themselves, others, and their learning experiences. Parents are considered an integral part of their children's education process."

CONTRA COSTA COUNTY
PRIVATE SECONDARY SCHOOLS

ANTIOCH CHRISTIAN TUTORIAL. See listing under Non-Catholic Religious Elementary Schools in Antioch.

ARLINGTON CHRISTIAN. See listing under Non-Catholic Religious Elementary Schools in Richmond.

THE ATHENIAN SCHOOL. 2100 Mt. Diablo, Danville 94526. (510) 837-5375. Eleanor Dase, Head of School. Christopher Beeson, Admissions. Est. 1965. Non-profit.

Gr. 6-12; 30 boarders, 270 day students.. $11,300, day students; $22,100, boarding. Inc. fees $1000. 23% receive fin. aid. 75 acre campus at base of Mt. Diablo. Avg. class size 15, max. 18. Spanish, French. 8 AP classes. Interdisciplinary and diverse course offerings. Wilderness experience, community service, town meetings, outdoor education, international exchange. Apply by Feb. 1; late applications accepted if space avail. Summer camp, summer school & ESL program. Accredited by WASC, member of CAIS.

98% of graduates go to 4 yr. colleges, 2% to 2 yr. SATs (100%): Class of '95, V 545, M 578; '94, V 532, M 574; '93 V 549, M 574. College counselor. In recent years, over 70% of Athenian's graduates have gained admission to their 1st choice school.

"The Athenian School provides a rigorous, innovative, and interdisciplinary college preparatory education. It prepares a diverse community of American and international students for the rigors of college and for lives of meaning and purpose."

BEREAN CHRISTIAN. 245 El Divisadero Ave., Walnut Creek 94598-4112. (510) 945-6464. Dr. Neil Sostrom, Director; Diane Shelloe, Admissions. Est. 1969. Non-profit.

Gr. 9-12; 250 students. Gr. 9 & 10, $3985; gr. 11 & 12, $4145. Reg. fee $125. 18% receive fin. aid. Closed campus. Avg. class size 17, max. 28. Spanish, French, 4 AP classes. Learning Center for students with limited learning dis-

129

abilities; on site LD specialist. College counselor. 60% of grads go to 4 yr. colleges, 40% to 2 yr. SAT scores (60-65%): Class of '94, V 451, M 480; '93, V 456, M 505. Accredited by WASC & ACSI.

Berean is "a Protestant Christian school which provides a quality education that compliments the values and beliefs of the home and church."

CARONDELET. 1133 Winton Dr., Concord 94518. (510) 686-5353. Catholic, girls. Gr. 9-12, 700 students.

CONTRA COSTA ALTERNATIVE SCHOOL. 10 Irwin Way, Orinda 94563. (510) 254-0199. Kate Knox, Director. Est. 1969. Non-profit.

Gr. 8-12 girls; gr. 9-12, boys; 40 students max. $5400-$9000 (sliding scale). 25% receive fin. aid. Avg. class size 7, max. 20. Closed campus. Arts & counseling oriented program. Ability grouping in academic classes. ADD & LD students accepted. College counselor, 25% of grads. attend 4 yr. colleges, 60% attend 2 yr. colleges. Apply any time. Accredited by Natl. Assoc. for Legal Support of Alternative Schools.

"We are a very small arts and counseling-oriented alternative high school. We will work with any student regardless of past academic performance, except for those with a history of violence."

CONTRA COSTA CHRISTIAN. 2721 Larkey Ln., Walnut Creek 94596. (510) 934-4964. N. Edmiston, Director. Jan Powers, Admissions. Est. 1979. Non-profit.

Gr. 9-12, 102 students. $4452-$5040. Inc. fees $280. Closed campus. Dress code. Avg. class size 16-20, max. 25. Spanish, French, 3 A.P. classes. On site L.D. specialist; resource room avail. at addtl. cost. College prep. courses, sports program. Apply by Aug. 15. Accredited by WASC.

College counselor. 86% of grads. go to 4 yr. colleges, 14% to 2 yr. SAT scores (70%): Class of '94, V 472, M 506; '93, V 499, M 478.

"Walnut Creek Christian Schools subscribe to a Christian philosophy of education based on God's truth as revealed in the Bible. We are dedicated to developing from a Christian perspective, our students' endowments for knowing, choosing and for acting."

DE LA SALLE. 1130 Winton Dr., Concord 94518. (510) 686-3310. Brother Robert J. Wickman, Principal. Est. 1965. Non-profit.

Boys, gr. 9-12, 900 students. $5300 + books. 10% receive fin. aid. Closed campus. Avg. class size 28, max. 32. Dress code. Honors classes & 7 AP classes. Spanish, French, Italian, Latin. College counselor. 68% of grads. attend 4 yr.

colleges, 30% 2 yr. Apply by the end of Jan. Waiting list. Summer program for incoming freshman. Accredited by WASC.

"De La Salle High School is a Roman Catholic educational community . . . which prepares students with varied academic needs and diverse social, cultural and economic backgrounds for college and life. . . Students are loved, instructed and guided according to the traditions of the Brothers of the Christian Schools. . .The promotion of a vital faith life, sponsorship of strong academic programs and a wide range of student activities. . . serve to educate students spiritually, intellectually, physically and socially in an environment that is moral, caring, and joyful. . .De La Salle also challenges them to . . . serve others, especially the poor and to deepen a sense of responsibility for humanity's future."

HERITAGE BAPTIST ACADEMY. See listing under Non-Catholic Religious Elementary Schools in Antioch.

HILLTOP SEVENTH DAY ADVENTIST CHRISTIAN. See listing under Non-Catholic Religious Elementary Schools in Antioch.

NORTH BAY ORINDA SCHOOL. 19 Altarinda Rd., Orinda 94563. (510) 254-7553. Ron Graydon, Director. Est. 1982. Non-profit.

Gr. 7-12; 97 students. $8200. Avg. class size 9, max. 15. Art, drama, chorus. Spanish & French, P.E., computers, typing, word processing. Many field trips; camping, skiing & river rafting trips. 40 hrs. of community service required for graduation. Bi-weekly progress reports; supervised study halls. Because of use of one-on-one instruction, we can effectively serve students with learning disabilities or A.D.D. but do not accept those with severe behavioral or emotional problems. College counselor. 65% of grads. go to 4 yr. colleges, 30% to 2 yr. colleges. Basketball team. 6 wk. summer program open to all students. Accredited by WASC.

We encourage a "very strong relationship and communication between teachers, parents and students through small classes and individualized programs....students, parents and teachers work together to create the optimal learning environment for each child."

PITTSBURG CHRISTIAN. 293 Alves Ln., Pittsburg 94565. (510) 458-1106.

SALESIAN. 2851 Salesian Ave., Richmond 94804. (510) 234-4433. Fr. John Itzaina, Principal. Ms. Dina Ward, Admissions. Est. as seminary in 1927, as school in 1960. Non-profit.

Gr. 9-12, 464 students. $4000. Reg. fee $400. 8% receive fin. aid. Closed campus. Dress code. Avg. class size 23, max. 35. Easy access by public transportation. Honors & 5 AP classes. Spanish & French. Students complete 20 hrs. community service/yr. Complete summer program. Placement exam for fall 9th grade given 1st Sat. in Feb. Accredited by WASC.

"The faculty and staff of Salesian High School endeavor to provide a college preparatory and comprehensive education to students from diverse socio-economic backgrounds. Recognizing the importance of sound, holistic education, we seek to nurture the physical, emotional, intellectual, social, moral and spiritual potential of our students."

SHORE ACRES CHRISTIAN. See listing under Non-Catholic Religious Elementary Schools in Pittsburg..

SPECTRUM CENTER VALLEY SCHOOL. See listing under Contra Costa County Special Education Schools.

CONTRA COSTA COUNTY PRIVATE SPECIAL EDUCATION SCHOOLS

CONTRA COSTA ALTERNATIVE. See listing under Contra Costa County Secondary Schools.

LA CHEIM. 1700 Oak Park Blvd., Bldg. D-1, Pleasant Hill 94523. (510) 930-7994. 2nd site at 5625 Sutter Ave., Richmond 94804. (510) 525-6882. Vic Prada, CEO. Joan Weill, Director of Pleasanton site; Charles Mason, Director of Richmond site. Est. 1974.

6-21 yrs. 100% funded by public school districts. Year-round school. Avg. class size 10, max. 12. Teacher student ratio 1:3. Structured program tailored to meet the academic, vocational, social and emotional needs of students with emotional, behavioral, and/or learning difficulties. Academic classes and on-going vocational education. Field trips, hot breakfast and lunch. Mental health staff offer individual, group, and family therapy. Certified by State Dept. of Ed. and accredited by WASC.

"La Cheim (To Life) is an environment designed to offer individualized tools and options to youngsters who are unable to succeed within the public school setting. The atmosphere provides opportunity for personal, academic, and social growth leading to a positive and life-giving sense of self. . . At La Cheim students develop confidence in their own abilities and begin to realize that they can be self-sufficient, caring, successful individuals. "

NEW VISTAS CHRISTIAN. 2073 Oak Park Blvd., Pleasant Hill 94523. (510) 930-8894. Linda Scott, Principal. Est. 1978. Non-profit.

K-gr. 8; 100 students. $6300-$6600. Inc. fees $300. 20% receive fin. aid. SDH: K, 8:30-12; gr. 1-6, 8:15-2:55; gr. 7-8, 8-3. EDC: 7 am-6 pm; $2.50/hr. Uniforms. Avg. & max. class size 12, classroom aides. All teachers are credentialed in special education. Afterschool flag football, soccer, softball, band, music, drama. Mandatory parent support meetings. Students must be diagnosed as learning disabled. Slingerland summer school; on campus training for teachers. Program for adults with L.D. Accredited by ACSI.

Our goal is "to provide bright, learning disabled children with special approaches and help that enable them to meet their full academic potential in a Christian atmosphere."

NORTH BAY ORINDA. See listing under Contra Costa County Secondary Schools.

SPRAINGS' ACADEMY. 89 Moraga Way, Orinda 94563. (510) 253-1906. Violet Spraings, PhD, Director. Est. 1967. Non-profit.

Ages 6-21 yrs. (adults also served on tutorial basis), 95 students. 45% funded by public schools. Avg. class size 6-8, max. 10. Teacher/student ratio 1:6. SDH: 8:30-2:30. Serves students with learning & language disabilities and ADD. It also serves students who are not learning disabled but need a small, structured environment in which to thrive. Reading, math, computer, & conceptual development lab. PE program, afterschool sports. College prep program; 60% of grads enter colleges & universities. Students admitted throughout the year. Summer programs. Accredited by CAPSES and certified by Calif. Dept. of Education.

"Every student can learn if given the appropriate input program & the circumstances & structure needed for learning."

SPECTRUM CENTER VALLEY SCHOOL. 1026 Oak Grove #1, Concord. (510) 685-9703. 545 Garretson St., Rodeo 94572. (510) 245-7036. Marilyn Coronado, Director. Est. 1975.

Ages 5-22 yrs.; 35 students at Concord Campus, 60 students at Rodeo campus. 100% funded through public schools. Avg. class size 8, max. 10. Teacher/student ratio 1:3 (or smaller). Spectrum serves students with severe developmental disabilities and challenging behaviors when there is no appropriate public school placement. Positive behavior intervention case manager, speech pathologists, special education teachers. 6 wk. extended year summer school. Certified by Calif. Dept. of Education.

"Spectrum Center's philosophy is based on the belief that all individuals have a right to an education which promotes independence to the greatest degree. The school program addresses student needs in areas of independent living, community integration, recreation, leisure & vocational training."

STARS SCHOOL 888 Podva Rd., Danville 94526. (510) 837-6040. James W. Partington, Ph. D & Mary Ann Powers, Ph.D, Directors. Est. 1991. Non-profit.

3-12 yrs; 18 students. 17% funded by public schools. Avg. class size 9, max. 10. Teacher/student ratio 1: 2 . SDH: 9-2. EDC: 8:30-4. School remains open 40 days in the summer. Certified by Calif. Dept. of Education.

STARS "seeks to provide high quality effective intervention for developmentally disabled and/or autistic children with intensive learning needs and to provide training for other professionals and parents in the delivery of these services."

APPENDIX

CALIFORNIA DISTINGUISHED
SCHOOL AWARDS

Since 1986 the State Department of Education has annually recognized schools to reward achievement and to motivate other schools to strive for excellence. Awards are given in alternate years to elementary and secondary schools. Because of budget cuts and the resulting suspension of state-wide testing, no awards were given in 1991.

Schools are selected for the award on the basis of a variety of indicators. Included in the Department of Education's lengthy list of characteristics that the 1995 schools had to demonstrate were:

- A meaning-centered, thinking curriculum focused on good literature;
- A safe, nurturing, child-centered environment free of drugs and crime;
- Families who participate in the educational process and daily life of the school;
- Exemplary measures of success, e.g., state and national tests, and statistics that demonstrate success in preventing vandalism, absenteeism and drop-outs;
- Use of community and business resources to enhance the curriculum and activities that link students and the school to the "real" world.
- Effective education of students who cannot speak English or who have physical or learning disabilities.

Not all schools, including many excellent ones, choose to apply for the award as the application is ten pages long and many schools choose not to expend their efforts on winning this kind of recognition. Because schools can no longer win in successive cycles, 1993 Distinguished Elementary Schools could not apply in 1995 but were asked to serve as mentors for newly applying schools. Once recognized as a "Distinguished School," no school loses the award. However, parents shouldn't assume that schools that received the award more than four years ago still offer the same quality of education that originally earned them recognition as outstanding schools.

ALAMEDA COUNTY
DISTINGUISHED SCHOOLS

DISTRICT	SCHOOL	YEAR
Alameda	Alameda H.S.	1992, 1994
Alameda	Chipman	1988
Alameda	Edison	1987
Alameda	Encinal H.S.	1994
Alameda	Haight	1989
Alameda	Lincoln Mid.	1992
Alameda	Lum	1987
Berkeley	Berkeley Arts Mag.	1989, 1993
Berkeley	Berkeley H.S.	1986
Berkeley	Jefferson	1995
Castro Valley	Castro Valley H.S.	1988
Castro Valley	Palomares	1989
Dublin	Dublin H.S.	1990, 1992
Dublin	Frederiksen	1995
Dublin	Nielsen	1993
Dublin	Wells Mid.	1994
Fremont	Blacow	1993
Fremont	Chadbourne	1993
Fremont	Durham, J. Haley	1993
Fremont	Grimmer	1993
Fremont	Hopkins J. H.	1992
Fremont	Irvington H.S.	1994
Fremont	Washington H.S.	1990
Hayward	Bowman	1987
Hayward	Glassbrook	1995
Hayward	Treeview	1995
Livermore Valley	East Ave. Mid.	1988
Livermore Valley	Junction Ave. Mid.	1988
New Haven	Alvarado	1986, 1994
New Haven	Barnard-White	1986, 1994
New Haven	Cabello	1993
New Haven	Decoto	1989, 1993
New Haven	Hillview Crest	1993
New Haven	Logan H.S.	1988, 1994
New Haven	New Haven Mid.	1994
New Haven	Pioneer	1987, 1993

DISTRICT	SCHOOL	YEAR
New Haven	Searles	1993
Newark	Newark J.H.	1988
Newark	Schilling	1995
Newark	Snow	1995
Oakland	Chabot	1989
Oakland	Cleveland	1989
Oakland	Crocker Highlands	1989
Oakland	Hillcrest	1993
Oakland	Miller	1989
Oakland	Roosevelt J.H.	1990
Oakland	Street Academy J.H.	1990
Oakland	Thornhill	1989
Piedmont	Beach	1989
Piedmont	Havens	1989
Piedmont	Piedmont H.S.	1992
Piedmont	Piedmont Mid.	1988, 1990
Pleasanton	Alisal	1989, 1995
Pleasanton	Amador Valley H.S.	1994
Pleasanton	Donlon	1995
Pleasanton	Fairlands	1995
Pleasanton	Foothill	1994
Pleasanton	Harvest Park Mid.	1994
Pleasanton	Lydiksen	1995
Pleasanton	Pleasanton Mid.	1994
Pleasanton	Vintage Hills	1995
San Leandro	Jefferson	1987
San Leandro	McKinley	1987
San Leandro	Roosevelt	1993
San Leandro	Washington	1987
San Lorenzo	Colonial Acres	1987
San Lorenzo	San Lorenzo H.S.	1991
Sunol Glen	Sunol Glen	1986

NATIONAL SCHOOL RECOGNITION PROGRAM

During the 1982-83 school year, the U.S. Department of Education established the Secondary School Recognition Program to identify private and public secondary schools that are exceptionally good at educating students. In the 1985-86 school year, the program was extended to include elementary schools and now alternates the awards between secondary and elementary schools each year.

The Chief School Officers of each state nominate public schools based on common criteria and guidelines developed by the U.S. Department of Education. The number of schools that may be nominated is equal to the size of the state's congressional delegation. The Council for American Private Education nominates private schools. A review panel screens the nominations and chooses the most promising schools for site visits. Site visitors observe the school and submit a report to the review panel which then makes recommendations to the U.S. Secretary of Education. Schools are evaluated on the basis of organization, leadership, curriculum, student achievement, character development, relations with the community, and efforts to maintain high quality programs. Secondary schools are also evaluated on student performance on standard achievement tests, a safe and drug free climate, success of students in post-secondary endeavors, number of disciplinary referrals, and dropout rates. The program looks for schools with an established record of sustained achievement and schools that have overcome obstacles and problems and are continuing to concentrate on improvement. Schools cannot receive the award in two consecutive cycles.

While winning a National Blue Ribbon award from the Department of Education is a great honor for a school, parents should realize that many excellent schools don't bother to apply. The application is 35 pages long and some districts feel that their energies and resources are better spent focusing on improving their students' education rather than getting recognition for what they do.

WINNERS OF NATIONAL SCHOOL RECOGNITION PROGRAM

SCHOOL	DISTRICT	YEAR
Alameda High	Alameda	1993
Alvarado Middle	New Haven	1984
Bishop O'Dowd	Catholic, Oakland	1991
Castro Valley High	Castro Valley	1985, 1989
Chadbourne	Fremont	1990
Durham, J. Haley	Fremont	1994
Gomes	Fremont	1988
Holy Names	Catholic, Oakland	1985, 1991
James Logan High	New Haven	1983, 1987
Mission San Jose High	Fremont	1987
Moreau Christian High	Christian—Hayward	1984, 1989
Piedmont High	Piedmont	1985
Pioneer Elem.	New Haven	1986
San Lorenzo High	San Lorenzo	1991
St. Elizabeth High	Catholic—Oakland	1984
St. Mary's College H.S.	Catholic—Berkeley	1985
Walters Jun. High	Fremont	1989

CONTRA COSTA COUNTY SCHOOLS

Alamo Elem.	San Ramon Valley	1986, 1992
Charlotte Wood Mid.	San Ramon Valley	1993
Country Club	San Ramon Valley	1994
Discovery Bay	Bryon Union	1986
Miramonte High	Acalanes Union	1987, 1991
Monte Gardens Elem.	Mt. Diablo	1992
St. David's Elem.	Catholic—Richmond	1986
St. John the Baptist	Catholic—El Cerrito	1988

EXPLANATION OF CLAS SCORES

After two years of development, with input from business leaders, educators, parents, testing experts and state officials, the California Learning Assessment System was given in 1993 and 1994 to the state's 4th, 8th and 10th graders to measure reading, writing, and math skills. It attempted to assess students' ability to think critically and creatively, to analyze and apply information, and to demonstrate a thorough understanding of the applicability of mathematical concepts. Instead of merely presenting students with multiple choice questions as traditional basic skills tests had done, the CLAS test also required students to perform tasks (e.g., write paragraphs and construct diagrams) to demonstrate their knowledge and understanding. The CLAS test evaluated student work according to performance levels ranging from 1 to 6. Each level for reading, writing, and math had defined characteristics. For example, a score of 1 on the reading level ". . . demonstrates no evidence of understanding a reading selection as a whole. . ." while a score of 6 "demonstrates a thorough. . .understanding of a reading selection. . .and makes effective use of evidence. . .to construct insightful and convincing interpretations or evaluations of its content and quality." Some critics argued that the tests could not be graded objectively; others questioned the content of some of the material on the reading tests and objected to students being asked to respond to how they felt about what they read. Defenders of the CLAS argue that for reform to occur in the classroom so that students will be prepared for the challenges of the modern workplace, multiple-choice assessments are no longer useful. Furthermore, most teachers who were involved in developing and scoring the CLAS tests felt that the experience helped them improve classroom instruction, focus on higher level thinking skills, and meet the goals of the state's curriculum frameworks.

In the fall of 1994, Governor Wilson, concerned that the CLAS tests had not yet generated individual student scores, vetoed the funding for the continuation of the CLAS test; therefore no state-wide assessment was given in 1995. It is likely that when a new one is developed, the new state assessment tool will reflect a middle ground between the objective, basic skills orientation of the old tests and the performance based test items that characterized the CLAS exam.

Note: Parents should always avoid making too much of test scores, especially when only one year's scores are available. For more on this subject, see "Answers to Frequently Asked Questions."

Explanation of CLAS table:

GR: grade level assessed.

SES: Socioeconomic status. The higher the value, the greater the socioeconomic status of the school population. At the elementary level, the SES is determined by the occupations of the parents. At the middle and high school level, the SES is determined by the educational background of the parents. A "1" is assigned to parents who didn't graduate from high school and a 5 to those who have an advanced degree.

%LEP: percentage of students designated as limited English proficient. LEP students who had been enrolled in school in the U.S. for fewer than 30 months or who were receiving instruction in a language other than English were not required to take the 1994 CLAS test.

% scoring 4+: The percentage of students achieving at or above performance level 4. (Those wishing to see the specific break down of how a school performed at each performance level, the science and history scores for grade five, or the descriptions of each performance level can contact their school district or order the complete CLAS results from the Department of Education by phoning 916-657-3011.)

C.G.: Next to each school's percentage of students scoring at 4 or above in each section of the CLAS exam is the percentage of those scoring 4 or above in the 100 schools most similar to the school. This comparison group was established on the basis of socioeconomic status, percent limited English proficient, student mobility, and percent of families receiving Aid to Families with Dependent Children. By comparing the two percentages, parents can get a better idea of how well a school is teaching the skills assessed by the CLAS exam when one takes into account the kind of population that a school serves.

1994 CLAS RESULTS

School	Gr.	SES	%LEP	% Scoring 4+					
				R	CG	WR	CG	M	CG
STATE	4	3.06	25	23	NA	32	NA	28	NA
	8	2.86	18	39	NA	46	NA	23	NA
	10	2.93	19	35	NA	39	NA	14	NA

ALAMEDA COUNTY CLAS SCORES

ALAMEDA UNIFIED SCHOOL DISTRICT

School	Gr.	SES	%LEP	R	CG	WR	CG	M	CG
ALAMEDA H.S.	10	3.43	27	44	46	52	49	27	22
BAY FARM	4	4.36	10	36	36	56	47	53	47
CHIPMAN	8	2.84	21	37	39	49	48	23	22
EARHART	4	3.97	16	53	36	61	46	66	46
EDISON	4	4.22	6	28	40	46	51	45	54
ENCINAL	10	3.08	27	37	41	40	44	16	17
HAIGHT	4	3.34	30	24	21	36	31	27	26
LINCOLN	8	3.68	9	57	59	67	64	54	42
LONGFELLOW	4	2.56	40	14	17	24	24	9	17
LUM	4	3.52	20	23	29	35	38	29	36
MILLER	4	3.15	9	11	26	32	36	17	34
OTIS	4	3.11	12	26	23	44	32	50	29
PADEN	4	3.64	7	34	29	51	39	42	41
WASHINGTON	4	3.04	19	24	21	28	29	43	26
WOOD	8	3.10	22	46	42	50	50	32	25
WOODSTOCK	4	3.32	16	20	24	35	35	23	31

ALBANY UNIFIED SCHOOL DISTRICT

School	Gr.	SES	%LEP	R	CG	WR	CG	M	CG
ALBANY H.S.	10	3.87	8	56	51	58	55	34	29
CORNELL	4	4.42	13	36	41	50	52	65	54
ALBANY MID.	8	4.05	7	66	66	54	71	45	50
MARIN	4	4.19	10	34	38	55	49	60	51

School	Gr.	SES	%LEP	R	CG	WR	CG	M	CG

BERKELEY UNIFIED SCHOOL DISTRICT

School	Gr.	SES	%LEP	R	CG	WR	CG	M	CG
ARTS MAGNET	4	3.55	6	3	27	17	37	35	39
BERKELEY H.S.	10	3.74	14	54	46	56	50	40	23
CRAGMONT/COLUMBUS	4	3.12	26	30	22	30	31	40	25
KING JR. H.	8	3.71	16	61	56	70	62	45	40
LONGFELLOW	4	3.58	5	30	21	37	30	33	25
MALCOLM X	4	3.62	6	28	23	39	31	44	28
MUIR	4	3.50	4	15	27	20	36	NA	40
WILLARD	8	3.52	7	51	44	56	52	36	28

CASTRO VALLEY UNIFIED SCHOOL DISTRICT

School	Gr.	SES	%LEP	R	CG	WR	CG	M	CG
CANYON MID.	8	3.57	0	55	48	65	56	35	32
CASTRO VALLEY	4	3.22	2	15	26	20	36	28	33
CASTRO VLLY. H.S.	10	3.53	1	43	42	55	49	19	21
CHABOT	4	4.00	0	45	36	45	46	47	50
INDEPENDENT	4	4.17	3	46	39	54	51	57	53
MARSHALL	4	3.63	0	28	29	31	40	29	39
PALOMARES	4	3.60	0	NA	23	NA	34	NA	34
PROCTOR	4	3.94	0	27	33	47	44	47	47
STANTON	4	3.30	4	50	27	38	39	46	35
VANNOY	4	4.22	2	52	39	60	51	65	54

DUBLIN UNIFIED SCHOOL DISTRICT

School	Gr.	SES	%LEP	R	CG	WR	CG	M	CG
DUBLIN H.S.	10	3.51	4	50	44	47	49	30	22
FREDERIKSEN	4	3.56	0	27	26	37	37	31	34
MURRAY	4	3.57	5	35	28	65	38	35	38
NEILSEN	4	4.33	0	44	40	53	50	66	55
WELLS MID.	8	3.39	3	57	52	62	58	35	34

EMERY UNIFIED SCHOOL DISTRICT

School	Gr.	SES	%LEP	R	CG	WR	CG	M	CG
EMERY H.S.	8	3.02	8	19	40	56	48	4	25
EMERY H.S.	10	2.86	9	28	25	29	30	3	10
YATES	4	2.69	15	26	16	15	25	15	20

FREMONT UNIFIED SCHOOL DISTRICT

School	Gr.	SES	%LEP	R	CG	WR	CG	M	CG
AMERICAN H.S.	10	3.30	16	22	42	28	46	13	20
ARDENWOOD	4	3.87	14	33	34	40	46	35	46
AZEVEDA	4	3.18	22	36	24	41	34	29	31

School	Gr.	SES	%LEP	% Scoring 4+					
				R	CG	WR	CG	M	CG
BLACOW	4	3.08	13	23	25	39	34	30	30
BRIER	4	2.92	11	27	23	39	33	38	28
BROOKVALE	4	3.91	5	29	34	46	44	33	46
CABRILLO	4	3.16	8	29	23	33	34	17	31
CENTERVILLE J. H.	8	3.31	7	42	48	40	57	26	32
CHADBOURNE	4	4.37	2	52	40	67	53	79	56
DURHAM	4	3.33	11	23	24	51	33	46	31
FOREST PARK	4	3.95	18	50	33	58	44	46	44
GLENMOOR	4	3.72	4	18	31	28	40	33	41
GOMES	4	4.43	1	41	43	57	54	66	57
GREEN	4	3.23	5	21	25	42	36	31	35
GRIMMER	4	2.62	38	17	18	36	27	25	22
HIRSCH	4	3.27	1	39	25	53	36	32	33
HOPKINS J.H.	8	4.15	3	69	60	74	67	61	45
HORNER J.H.	8	3.23	5	44	46	69	55	38	29
IRVINGTON H.S.	10	3.35	6	45	42	43	47	23	20
KENNEDY H.S.	10	3.19	27	33	40	49	43	22	18
MALONEY	4	3.75	8	24	30	31	40	35	39
MATTOS	4	3.42	10	31	25	35	37	39	35
MILLARD	4	3.41	6	23	28	36	39	34	37
MISSION SAN JOSE	10	4.12	4	65	51	69	55	38	27
MISSION SAN JOSE	4	4.05	3	35	37	61	48	43	51
MISSION VALLEY	4	3.91	2	31	35	60	46	56	48
NILES	4	3.71	10	31	32	58	44	57	45
OLIVEIRA	4	3.51	6	18	28	36	38	25	37
PARKMONT	4	3.45	3	36	28	48	38	30	38
PATTERSON	4	3.27	31	22	23	27	33	20	27
THORTON J.H.	8	3.18	14	44	47	55	56	29	29
VALLEJO MILL	4	3.46	26	32	25	49	35	20	32
WALTERS J.H.	8	3.03	15	44	44	64	53	28	27
WARM SPRINGS	4	3.92	8	32	34	46	45	42	44
WARWICK	4	3.41	9	27	27	37	38	30	34
WASHINGTON H.S.	10	3.60	6	33	44	43	49	16	22
WEIBEL	4	4.89	2	49	43	51	56	62	60

HAYWARD UNIFIED SCHOOL DISTRICT

School	Gr.	SES	%LEP	R	CG	WR	CG	M	CG
BOWMAN	4	2.70	20	33	18	24	26	24	20
BRET HARTE INT.	8	3.24	6	36	46	60	54	25	29
BURBANK	4	2.25	47	18	16	28	24	19	17
CHERRYLAND	4	2.70	21	15	18	16	25	22	18
EAST AVENUE	4	3.98	4	43	36	43	48	57	50
EDEN	4	3.13	27	34	21	50	31	38	27
EDEN GARDENS	4	3.34	17	21	26	39	36	29	32

School	Gr.	SES	%LEP	% Scoring 4+					
				R	CG	WR	CG	M	CG
ELDRIDGE	4	3.12	44	12	20	20	29	30	24
FAIRVIEW	4	3.32	13	26	23	35	33	19	30
HARDER	4	2.84	18	8	18	19	27	23	21
HAYWARD H.S.	10	3.01	18	36	36	42	40	15	14
HIGHLAND	4	3.17	7	32	25	52	36	41	32
KING, MRTN. LTHR.	8	2.84	32	27	35	41	44	18	19
LA VISTA INT.	8	2.49	28	30	32	45	41	13	17
LONGWOOD	4	2.48	40	14	16	17	26	15	19
MARKHAM	4	3.42	15	17	23	8	34	0	31
MT. EDEN H.S.	10	2.92	27	32	36	36	39	18	14
MUIR	4	3.15	30	11	21	19	28	8	22
OCHOA	8	2.95	21	40	42	55	50	23	24
PALMA CEIA	4	3.30	27	20	25	19	35	14	33
PARK	4	2.95	23	24	22	48	32	33	27
RUUS	4	2.96	35	19	20	30	30	21	23
SCHAFER PARK	4	3.16	14	15	24	39	35	41	32
SOUTHGATE	4	2.94	19	16	21	32	32	33	27
STROBRIDGE	4	2.51	14	18	20	30	28	31	27
TENNYSON H.S.	10	2.71	33	14	32	23	35	5	11
TREEVIEW	4	3.00	10	15	19	31	29	14	25
TYRRELL	4	2.63	49	17	14	17	21	18	13
WINTON INT.	8	2.36	21	36	29	49	39	15	15

LIVERMORE VALLEY JOINT UNION SCHOOL DISTRICT

School	Gr.	SES	%LEP	R	CG	WR	CG	M	CG
ARROYO SECO	4	3.82	2	25	33	39	43	46	45
CHRISTENSEN	4	3.61	3	17	29	39	40	40	38
CHRISTENSEN	8	3.26	2	53	49	75	55	32	31
EAST AVE. MIDDLE	8	3.39	5	51	51	61	56	39	33
GRANADA H.S.	10	3.55	3	41	43	54	49	NA	22
JACKSON AVE.	4	3.72	12	28	30	47	41	33	39
JUNCTION AVE. MID.	8	3.20	5	43	47	59	54	34	29
LIVERMORE H.S.	10	3.49	6	33	43	43	48	16	21
MARYLIN AVE.	4	3.34	13	19	25	28	35	19	32
MENDENHALL MID.	8	3.82	1	63	59	57	64	51	42
MICHELL	4	3.32	3	37	26	48	38	32	37
PORTOLA	4	3.01	13	17	22	31	33	36	28
RANCHO LAS POS.	4	3.53	1	19	29	27	39	30	38
SMITH	4	4.20	0	42	38	56	51	56	54
SUNSET	4	4.10	0	36	36	50	48	57	51

School	Gr.	SES	%LEP	% Scoring 4+					
				R	CG	WR	CG	M	CG

MOUNTAIN HOUSE ELEMENTARY SCHOOL DISTRICT

School	Gr.	SES	%LEP	% Scoring 4+					
MOUNTAIN HOUSE	4	3.00	0	NO SCORES AVAILABLE					
MOUNTAIN HOUSE	8	3.00	14	NO SCORES AVAILABLE					

NEW HAVEN UNIFIED SCHOOL DISTRICT

School	Gr.	SES	%LEP	R	CG	WR	CG	M	CG
ALVARADO	4	2.80	26	40	23	43	31	48	26
ALVARADO MID.	8	3.33	16	54	48	78	56	24	32
BARNARD-WHITE	8	2.85	15	55	40	65	48	24	23
CABELLO	4	3.06	26	41	22	39	31	41	27
DECOTO	4	2.51	26	15	18	20	27	31	21
HILLVIEW CREST	4	2.67	19	36	23	39	33	42	27
LOGAN H.S.	10	3.10	19	30	34	45	37	11	13
NEW HAVEN MID.	8	3.18	13	48	46	67	54	24	29
PIONEER	4	3.41	23	43	28	46	37	61	34
SEARLES	4	2.81	22	33	23	47	32	41	27

NEWARK UNIFIED SCHOOL DISTRICT

School	Gr.	SES	%LEP	R	CG	WR	CG	M	CG
BUNKER	4	3.59	0	15	28	34	38	37	39
GRAHAM	4	2.79	23	11	21	26	30	31	25
KENNEDY	4	3.08	1	30	25	16	35	42	32
LINCOLN	4	3.64	1	21	29	28	39	36	39
MILANI	4	3.35	14	19	25	20	35	35	32
MUSICK	4	3.33	5	16	26	14	37	23	35
NEWARK JR. H.	8	2.98	3	40	41	51	50	21	25
NEWARK MEM.	10	2.98	10	40	35	44	41	12	14
SCHILLING	4	3.04	8	23	21	44	31	43	27
SNOW	4	3.25	8	23	23	53	35	33	32

OAKLAND UNIFIED SCHOOL DISTRICT

School	Gr.	SES	%LEP	R	CG	WR	CG	M	CG
ALLENDALE	4	2.41	33	17	14	20	20	12	14
BELLA VISTA	4	2.22	68	16	11	20	18	7	11
BREWER JR. H.	8	2.54	31	26	31	35	40	22	16
BROOKFIELD VIL.	4	2.30	7	3	12	9	19	2	12
BURBANK	4	1.77	1	0	13	9	20	0	14
BURCKHALTER	4	1.41	8	23	18	11	27	18	22
CARTER MID.	8	2.95	9	21	24	33	30	5	11
CASTLEMONT H.S.	10	2.54	16	26	24	24	28	1	8
CHABOT	4	3.93	4	40	34	52	44	52	47
CLAREMONT MID.	8	3.27	7	40	48	51	56	26	31

School	Gr.	SES	%LEP	% Scoring 4+					
				R	CG	WR	CG	M	CG
CLEVELAND	4	2.91	19	40	13	66	20	46	13
COLE	4	1.41	1	9	13	2	20	8	14
COX	4	2.00	26	16	14	21	20	5	14
CROCKER	4	3.84	4	32	34	34	45	37	46
ELMHURST MID.	8	2.47	19	17	24	31	30	2	10
EMERSON	4	3.08	13	23	15	32	22	16	16
FOSTER MID.	8	2.65	12	19	24	14	30	6	11
FRANKLIN	4	1.76	69	18	12	14	18	14	11
FREMONT H.S.	10	2.00	65	13	27	17	31	2	9
FRICK JR. H.	8	2.61	10	12	24	10	30	9	11
FRUITVALE	4	2.45	39	14	16	17	23	15	16
GARFIELD	4	2.15	75	6	13	14	19	8	11
GLENVIEW	4	2.59	18	23	20	34	29	26	23
GOLDEN GATE	4	2.00	0	0	13	9	20	3	16
GRASS VALLEY	4	3.42	0	15	22	42	31	28	33
HARTE, BRET	8	3.12	18	30	44	39	51	15	27
HAVENSCOURT	8	1.99	41	16	24	17	30	7	10
HAWTHORNE	4	2.49	65	5	13	13	21	2	11
HIGHLAND	4	2.24	35	9	12	15	18	1	11
HILLCREST	4	4.55	0	55	43	70	54	77	60
HOOVER	4	2.10	20	8	12	22	18	15	12
HOWARD	4	3.5	5	17	25	30	36	16	35
JEFFERSON	4	2.24	65	7	12	14	20	6	10
KAISER	4	3.76	3	10	29	59	40	41	44
KAISER	8	3.90	0	73	61	78	66	50	44
KING ESTATES JR. H.	8	2.90	2	9	40	11	47	9	22
LA ESCUELITA	4	2.68	57	13	16	36	23	16	19
LAFAYETTE	4	2.40	2	9	14	11	23	4	17
LAKEVIEW	4	2.35	5	11	17	18	25	11	21
LAUREL	4	2.99	27	24	21	56	30	32	24
LAZEAR	4	2.59	66	4	16	9	22	7	16
LINCOLN	4	2.52	67	21	16	31	23	31	17
LOCKWOOD	4	1.82	38	10	11	14	17	6	10
LONGFELLOW	4	1.72	8	9	12	15	18	2	12
LOWELL MID.	8	2.58	12	13	25	16	32	2	11
MADISON MID.	8	2.35	15	24	24	21	30	3	11
MANN	4	2.32	27	18	13	18	19	7	12
MANZANITA	4	2.05	51	7	12	13	18	6	12
MARKHAM	4	2.50	15	8	12	8	18	3	12
MARSHALL	4	3.56	1	2	28	19	40	7	38
MAXWELL PARK	4	3.22	6	11	22	15	30	8	28
MCCLYMONDS H.S.	10	2.70	4	14	24	29	28	0	8
MELROSE	4	2.24	57	2	15	13	22	0	14
MILLER	4	4.59	0	62	46	64	57	70	63

School	Gr.	SES	%LEP	% Scoring 4+					
				R	CG	WR	CG	M	CG
MONTCLAIR	4	4.52	0	52	44	54	54	44	60
MONTERA JR. H.	8	3.98	3	58	61	57	67	41	45
MUNCK	4	3.91	2	31	36	45	46	26	47
OAKLAND H.S.	10	2.06	39	23	28	32	31	9	8
OAKLAND TECH.	10	2.84	20	26	28	37	32	7	10
PARKER	4	1.64	1	7	14	23	22	10	16
PERALTA	4	3.47	0	16	24	11	35	21	35
PIEDMONT AVE.	4	2.03	12	13	15	23	23	8	18
PRESCOTT	4	2.09	27	20	13	15	19	7	12
REDWOOD HEIGHTS	4	3.95	0	46	34	37	46	35	46
ROOSEVELT JR. H.	8	1.92	58	26	24	23	30	6	10
SANTA FE	4	2.36	6	11	12	25	19	6	12
SEQUOIA	4	3.35	9	18	25	28	35	28	32
SHERMAN	4	3.37	2	11	21	22	31	0	28
SIMMONS JR. H.	8	2.14	45	20	24	18	31	4	11
SKYLINE H.S.	10	3.03	16	29	36	36	41	10	15
SOBRANTE PARK	4	2.52	26	3	13	12	19	6	13
STONEHURST	4	2.26	42	16	15	13	21	9	14
SWETT	4	3.88	6	14	31	33	42	19	42
THORNHILL	4	4.32	5	63	42	65	53	70	57
WASHINGTON	4	2.59	3	11	15	15	23	11	17
WEBSTER ACDMY.	4	2.14	24	9	12	13	18	7	11
WESTLAKE JR. H.	8	2.70	23	28	35	39	43	10	19
WHITTIER	4	1.82	45	19	11	20	17	2	10

PIEDMONT UNIFIED SCHOOL DISTRICT

BEACH	4	4.41	7	54	42	52	53	81	57
HAVENS	4	4.99	2	53	46	65	58	81	65
PIEDMONT H.S.	10	4.49	2	57	54	57	58	40	32
PIEDMONT MID.	8	4.64	0	83	69	88	74	71	55
WILDWOOD	4	4.75	7	33	46	41	58	70	62

PLEASANTON UNIFIED SCHOOL DISTRICT

ALISAL	4	4.08	0	43	37	50	47	50	48
AMADOR VLLY.	10	3.95	1	50	48	62	54	25	25
DONLON	4	4.45	1	46	38	54	49	58	50
FAIRLANDS	4	4.07	2	30	35	48	46	53	46
FOOTHILL H.S.	10	3.68	0	66	44	79	50	28	23
HARVEST PARK MID.	8	3.9	0	71	59	88	65	46	43
LYDIKSEN	4	4.58	2	43	45	68	55	60	60
PLEASANTON MID.	8	3.76	0	65	54	74	62	51	37
VALLEY VIEW	4	4.15	1	49	34	62	45	47	46

School	Gr.	SES	%LEP	% Scoring 4+					
				R	CG	WR	CG	M	CG
VINTAGE HILLS	4	4.13	1	40	37	61	49	50	51
WALNUT GROVE	4	4.64	0	37	40	53	52	60	53

SAN LEANDRO UNIFIED SCHOOL DISTRICT

School	Gr.	SES	%LEP	R	CG	WR	CG	M	CG
BANCROFT MIDDLE	8	3.2	9	35	49	39	56	25	30
GARFIELD	4	3.03	27	18	22	30	31	27	24
JEFFERSON	4	3.41	14	50	20	39	29	62	26
MCKINLEY	4	3.16	9	23	25	37	35	26	32
MONROE	4	3.74	8	36	28	39	39	29	38
MUIR MIDDLE	8	2.74	16	45	40	67	48	22	22
ROOSEVELT	4	4.06	4	37	36	43	46	61	50
SAN LEANDRO H.S.	10	3.13	12	33	39	37	44	13	17
WASHINGTON	4	3.26	20	44	24	53	34	45	33
WILSON	4	3.09	26	20	22	28	32	13	26

SAN LORENZO UNIFIED SCHOOL DISTRICT

School	Gr.	SES	%LEP	R	CG	WR	CG	M	CG
ARROYO H.S.	8	2.84	7	42	41	48	50	22	25
ARROYO H.S.	10	2.85	14	56	37	57	41	18	15
BAY	4	3.21	7	23	25	28	37	37	33
COLONIAL ACRES	4	3.16	16	11	23	19	32	20	29
CORVALLIS	4	3.67	12	18	29	37	40	17	38
DEL REY	4	3.59	4	30	28	25	40	35	37
EDENDALE	4	3.01	29	15	21	24	28	26	23
HESPERIAN	4	3.11	22	15	20	28	30	24	24
HILLSIDE	4	2.53	27	2	17	5	25	19	19
LORENZO MANOR	4	2.99	20	24	22	32	32	28	27
SAN LORENZO H.S.	8	2.69	8	33	35	46	44	19	19
SAN LORENZO H.S.	10	2.80	15	41	36	51	40	15	13
WASHINGTON MANOR	4	3.35	18	20	26	34	36	32	32

SUNOL GLEN UNIFIED SCHOOL DISTRICT

School	Gr.	SES	%LEP	R	CG	WR	CG	M	CG
SUNOL GLEN	4	3.90	0	52	32	39	42	NA	45
SUNOL GLEN	8	3.70	0	71	50	57	58	52	33

CONTRA COSTA
COUNTY CLAS SCORES

School	Gr.	SES	%LEP	% Scoring 4+					
				R	CG	WR	CG	M	CG

ACALANES UNION HIGH SCHOOL DISTRICT

School	Gr.	SES	%LEP	R	CG	WR	CG	M	CG
ACALANES H.S.	10	4.46	0	70	54	67	58	49	31
CAMPOLINDO	10	4.35	1	73	54	70	58	43	31
LAS LOMAS H.S.	10	4.00	10	63	52	68	57	34	30
MIRAMONTE H.S.	10	4.37	0	75	54	69	58	41	31

ANTIOCH UNIFIED SCHOOL DISTRICT

School	Gr.	SES	%LEP	R	CG	WR	CG	M	CG
ANTIOCH H.S.	10	3.10	2	43	35	43	40	17	14
ANTIOCH JR. H.	8	2.94	3	43	40	52	48	22	23
BELSHAW	4	3.41	2	21	27	33	36	35	35
BIDWELL	4	3.55	3	35	28	38	38	36	38
FREMONT	4	2.45	8	13	18	23	26	14	21
JACK LONDON	4	3.63	2	30	28	39	38	45	36
KIMBALL	4	3.05	5	13	24	22	33	19	32
MARSH	4	2.74	12	15	19	22	27	19	22
MISSION	4	3.19	2	23	21	31	29	20	24
MUIR	4	3.97	3	34	32	35	43	36	42
PARK JR. H.	8	3.20	2	51	43	52	51	25	26
SUTTER	4	3.66	0	15	28	25	39	27	37
TURNER	4	3.42	5	25	23	27	33	30	28

BRENTWOOD UNION SCHOOL DISTRICT

School	Gr.	SES	%LEP	R	CG	WR	CG	M	CG
BRENTWOOD	4	3.29	4	22	25	37	34	25	33
EDNA HILL MID.	8	2.94	11	52	41	58	50	19	23
GARIN	4	3.21	24	40	23	48	33	41	27
NUNN	4	3.9	0	25	34	26	44	41	47

School	Gr.	SES	%LEP	% Scoring 4+					
				R	CG	WR	CG	M	CG

BRYON UNION ELEMENTARY SCHOOL DISTRICT

School	Gr.	SES	%LEP	R	CG	WR	CG	M	CG
BRYON	8	3.47	4	41	46	55	53	19	30
DISCOVERY BAY	4	3.12	3	22	24	25	34	25	31

CANYON ELEMENTARY SCHOOL DISTRICT

School	Gr.	SES	%LEP						
CANYON	4	3.85	0	NO SCORES AVAILABLE					

JOHN SWETT UNIFIED SCHOOL DISTRICT

School	Gr.	SES	%LEP	R	CG	WR	CG	M	CG
CARQUINEZ MIDDLE	8	3.30	4	48	43	65	49	18	27
HILLCREST	4	3.06	8	16	21	22	29	30	24
SWETT H.S.	10	3.11	4	52	33	53	39	17	15

KNIGHTSEN ELEMENTARY SCHOOL DISTRICT

School	Gr.	SES	%LEP	R	CG	WR	CG	M	CG
KNIGHTSEN	4	2.53	0	6	20	6	29	3	25
KNIGHTSEN	8	2.48	6	59	40	61	47	36	22

LAFAYETTE ELEMENTARY SCHOOL DISTRICT

School	Gr.	SES	%LEP	R	CG	WR	CG	M	CG
BURTON VALLEY	4	4.69	1	54	42	65	53	75	55
HAPPY VALLEY	4	4.77	0	61	46	64	58	69	64
LAFAYETTE	4	4.26	3	37	40	43	53	50	55
STANLEY INT.	8	4.31	0	73	66	80	71	61	51
SPRINGHILL	4	4.52	0	42	44	58	55	64	60

LIBERTY UNION HIGH SCHOOL DISTRICT

School	Gr.	SES	%LEP	R	CG	WR	CG	M	CG
LIBERTY H.S.	10	2.93	11	42	35	34	40	12	13

MARTINEZ UNIFIED SCHOOL DISTRICT

School	Gr.	SES	%LEP	R	CG	WR	CG	M	CG
ALHAMBRA H.S.	10	3.28	8	32	37	40	41	19	17
JOHN SWETT	4	3.38	0	47	23	59	33	51	32
LAS JUNTAS	4	3.54	3	12	27	37	37	22	35
MARTINEZ JR. H.	8	3.20	4	51	46	71	54	34	29
MORELLO PARK	4	3.91	3	29	34	42	46	38	46
MUIR	4	3.29	1	18	25	25	35	24	34

School	Gr.	SES	%LEP	R	CG	WR	CG	M	CG

% Scoring 4+

MORAGA ELEMENTRAY SCH0OL DISTRICT

School	Gr.	SES	%LEP	R	CG	WR	CG	M	CG
CAMINO PABLO	4	4.60	2	43	44	64	54	71	59
MORAGA INT.	8	4.44	2	74	69	79	74	63	54
RHEEM	4	4.47	2	48	43	71	54	70	58

MT. DIABLO UNIFIED SCHOOL DISTRICT

School	Gr.	SES	%LEP	R	CG	WR	CG	M	CG
AYERS	4	3.48	2	15	26	26	37	18	36
BANCROFT	4	4.17	3	49	37	62	48	71	51
BEL AIR	4	2.93	14	6	19	18	28	9	24
CLAYTON VALLEY	10	3.62	2	40	45	24	51	22	23
COLLEGE PARK H.S.	10	3.72	2	60	45	58	52	30	23
CONCORD H.S.	10	3.26	6	56	40	46	45	18	18
EL DORADO INT.	8	3.36	6	60	48	65	57	40	33
EL MONTE	4	3.39	2	17	23	43	33	36	30
FAIR OAKS	4	3.10	11	18	21	29	29	20	25
FOOTHILL MID.	8	4.23	3	75	64	77	70	59	48
GLENBROOK MID.	8	2.73	17	35	36	43	45	13	19
HIDDEN VALLEY	4	4.00	2	22	33	39	44	40	44
HIGHLANDS	4	3.87	4	24	33	34	44	37	44
HOLBROOK	4	2.72	8	8	19	5	28	18	24
MEADOW HOMES	4	2.71	40	29	18	37	27	23	19
MONTE GARDENS	4	3.49	1	42	29	58	38	50	38
MOUNTAIN VIEW	4	3.59	7	32	29	29	40	47	39
MT. DIABLO	4	4.09	0	42	36	49	47	50	48
MT. DIABLO H.S.	10	2.74	20	34	32	34	36	9	12
NORTHGATE H.S.	10	4.26	3	62	53	68	57	33	30
OAK GROVE MID.	8	3.39	8	49	50	57	57	32	33
PINE HOLLOW INT.	8	3.48	3	48	49	61	58	36	33
PLEASANT HILL	4	3.84	3	31	33	35	43	50	43
RIO VISTA	4	2.65	16	18	20	23	27	32	23
RIVERVIEW MID.	8	2.86	16	23	38	41	46	14	21
SEQUOIA	4	3.98	5	55	36	56	47	60	49
SEQUOIA MID.	8	3.74	0	68	54	66	60	56	38
SHORE ACRES	4	2.54	34	10	18	15	27	4	19
SILVERWOOD	4	3.50	6	14	25	48	37	32	35
STRANDWOOD	4	3.68	9	29	30	41	40	49	39
SUN TERRACE	4	2.94	7	24	21	26	30	21	27
VALHALLA	4	3.88	2	24	34	45	45	40	46
VALLE VERDE	4	4.04	2	51	36	57	48	63	49
VALLEY VIEW	8	3.40	3	59	48	81	56	39	32
WALNUT ACRES	4	4.13	3	51	35	60	46	58	47

School	Gr.	SES	%LEP	% Scoring 4+					
				R	CG	WR	CG	M	CG
WESTWOOD	4	3.02	3	34	23	31	34	28	30
WOODSIDE	4	3.66	2	31	31	50	41	65	40
WREN AVE.	4	2.86	7	12	21	25	30	25	26
YGNACIO H.S.	10	3.40	10	32	43	29	47	14	21
YGNACIO VALLEY	4	3.06	34	18	21	16	29	13	23

OAKLEY UNION ELEMENTARY SCHOOL DISTRICT

School	Gr.	SES	%LEP	R	CG	WR	CG	M	CG
GEHRINGER	4	3.04	5	15	22	30	31	35	27
LAUREL	4	3.59	6	17	30	35	41	42	39
O'HARA PARK MID.	8	3.01	5	22	44	28	52	11	26
OAKLEY	4	2.94	4	9	22	12	32	14	28
VINTAGE PARKWAY	4	3.10	1	30	24	36	33	30	31

ORINDA UNION ELEMENTARY SCHOOL DISTRICT

School	Gr.	SES	%LEP	R	CG	WR	CG	M	CG
DEL REY	4	4.72	0	51	45	55	57	83	63
GLORIETTA	4	4.81	0	42	45	66	57	64	63
ORINDA INT.	8	4.49	0	74	69	79	74	63	54
SLEEPY HOLLOW	4	4.86	0	40	47	56	58	71	64

PITTSBURG UNIFIED SCHOOL DISTRICT

School	Gr.	SES	%LEP	R	CG	WR	CG	M	CG
CENTRAL JR. H.	8	2.60	13	33	34	39	42	14	18
FOOTHILL	4	2.56	25	25	18	36	26	19	19
HEIGHTS	4	2.96	17	16	19	24	28	19	22
HIGHLANDS	4	2.99	13	15	19	23	27	12	22
HILLVIEW JR. H.	8	2.86	0	44	39	43	46	18	22
LOS MEDANOS	4	2.84	25	21	18	45	27	34	22
PARKSIDE	4	2.66	34	24	18	22	27	39	19
PITTSBURG H.S.	10	2.98	8	42	33	49	39	14	13
STONEMAN	4	3.21	11	16	27	31	36	29	34
VILLAGE	4	2.61	16	8	17	12	26	13	20

SAN RAMON VALLEY UNIFIED SCHOOL DISTRICT

School	Gr.	SES	%LEP	R	CG	WR	CG	M	CG
ALAMO	4	4.56	0	44	44	62	46	56	62
ARMSTRONG	4	4.00	4	47	36	58	47	57	50
BALDWIN	4	4.64	2	48	44	62	55	65	61
BOLLINGER CANYON	4	4.27	2	48	39	60	50	55	53
CALIFORNIA H.S.	10	3.85	0	62	46	65	53	30	24
COUNTRY CLUB	4	4.17	1	51	35	67	48	63	49
DISNEY	4	3.92	5	50	35	51	46	72	47
GOLDEN VIEW	4	4.43	1	56	41	65	51	55	56

School	Gr.	SES	%LEP	R	CG	WR	CG	M	CG
						% Scoring 4+			
GREEN VALLEY	4	3.63	0	50	29	62	40	60	38
GREENBROOK	4	4.15	1	51	37	59	47	57	48
LOS CERROS MID.	8	4.33	1	62	65	74	71	48	50
MONTAIR	4	4.58	0	58	44	48	53	66	59
MONTE VISTA H.S.	10	4.27	1	48	52	46	57	33	29
MONTEVIDEO	4	4.58	1	42	45	47	57	42	62
PINE VALLEY INT.	8	3.92	0	58	56	68	64	43	41
RANCHO ROMERO	4	4.49	1	59	43	66	54	67	58
SAN RAMON VLLY.	10	4.14	0	44	51	64	56	21	28
STONE VALLEY INT.	8	4.22	0	86	68	89	73	69	52
SYCAMORE VALLEY	4	4.76	0	79	43	77	54	80	58
TWIN CREEKS	4	4.08	0	40	37	66	48	66	52
VISTA GRANDE	4	4.47	0	42	42	53	54	71	56
WOOD INT.	8	4.11	0	66	63	68	68	45	47

WALNUT CREEK ELEMENTARY SCHOOL DISTRICT

School	Gr.	SES	%LEP	R	CG	WR	CG	M	CG
BUENA VISTA	4	3.87	10	48	36	60	47	60	46
INDIAN VALLEY	4	3.93	1	44	35	67	46	60	49
MURWOOD	4	4.00	1	44	36	64	48	61	49
PARKMEAD	4	4.25	1	46	39	59	51	71	55
WALNUT CREEK INT.	8	3.97	1	70	62	77	68	60	46
WALNUT HEIGHTS	4	4.33	1	38	42	53	53	53	58

WEST CONTRA COSTA UNIFIED SCHOOL DISTRICT

School	Gr.	SES	%LEP	R	CG	WR	CG	M	CG
ADAMS MID.	8	3.49	7	44	51	54	58	33	34
BAYVIEW	4	2.55	31	10	18	5	27	11	21
CASTRO	4	2.74	3	15	22	17	32	28	29
COLLINS	4	3.18	6	18	24	26	34	30	33
CORONADO	4	1.58	22	0	13	3	20	0	14
CRESPI JR. H.	8	2.96	14	35	39	48	48	16	23
DE ANZA H.S.	10	3.10	9	25	35	36	41	11	15
DOVER	4	1.83	61	8	14	12	22	12	14
DOWNER	4	2.46	59	6	15	11	24	7	14
EL CERRITO H.S.	10	3.47	6	37	38	48	42	20	18
EL SOBRANTE	4	3.23	9	31	22	18	32	28	28
ELLERHORST	4	4.02	5	22	36	32	47	29	51
FAIRMONT	4	3.51	24	15	25	21	35	24	31
FORD	4	2.65	23	9	17	12	24	5	18
GRANT	4	1.23	38	10	15	8	23	5	17
HARDING	4	3.28	2	28	27	37	37	22	36
HELMS MID.	8	2.13	35	8	25	17	32	5	12
HERCULES	4	3.54	9	10	28	9	39	18	37

School	Gr.	SES	%LEP	% Scoring 4+					
				R	CG	WR	CG	M	CG
HIGHLAND	4	2.32	30	3	15	5	22	7	15
KENNEDY H.S.	10	2.91	22	9	28	27	31	6	10
KENSINGTON	4	4.40	1	58	40	68	53	80	57
KING	4	2.51	22	11	13	9	19	0	13
LAKE	4	3.10	42	5	15	29	23	11	16
LINCOLN	4	2.06	57	3	16	11	24	2	15
MADERA	4	4.09	3	36	38	46	49	52	50
MIDDLE COLLEGE H.S.	10	3.28	6	43	39	55	43	9	17
MIRA VISTA	4	3.18	9	6	23	8	35	8	33
MONTALVIN MANOR	4	3.00	23	11	18	18	25	16	21
MURPHY	4	2.32	6	11	19	19	29	10	25
NYSTROM	4	1.94	5	8	12	0	19	2	13
OHLONE	4	3.87	13	NA	36	NA	46	NA	47
OLINDA	4	3.58	10	29	30	32	40	34	39
PERES	4	2.85	25	5	13	6	19	12	13
PINOLE JR. H.	8	3.27	5	37	45	46	54	19	29
PINOLE VALLEY H.S.	10	3.38	9	41	40	54	46	20	19
PORTOLA JR. H.	8	2.88	10	14	36	22	44	13	20
RICHMOND H.S.	10	1.98	49	24	26	24	30	4	8
RIVERSIDE	4	2.94	11	0	19	6	28	9	24
SEAVIEW	4	3.44	10	32	27	30	38	31	39
SHANNON	4	2.65	13	13	22	17	33	18	27
SHELDON	4	3.51	7	38	27	43	37	48	35
STEGE	4	2.36	17	12	13	8	19	4	12
STEWART	4	3.61	4	16	29	33	40	28	40
TARA HILLS	4	3.07	7	32	23	26	34	22	31
VALLEY VIEW	4	3.84	3	66	34	54	44	51	45
VERDE	4	1.77	23	8	12	4	18	4	14
WASHINGTON	4	3.18	11	9	22	14	31	0	27
WILSON	4	3.27	14	21	22	24	32	16	29

HIGH SCHOOL
PERFORMANCE REPORTS

In November of 1994, the California Department of Education released performance reports for every high school in the state. The report was based on data gathered in the 1992-93 school year. The average performance value was based on a number of indicators: 10th grade CLAS test results, geometry enrollment rates, a-f course (subjects accepted by University of California as requirements for admission) enrollment & completion rates, drop-out rates, UC & CSU attendance rates, SAT & ACT scores, and Advanced Placement test results. Listed below is the average performance value for each comprehensive high school and the average performance value for each school's comparison group—the 100 schools in the state most demographically similar. Factors used in forming comparison groups include the percentage of students who have limited English proficiency, the percentage of students from families receiving AFDC, student mobility, and socio-economic status as measured by parental education. To obtain a breakdown of the individual indicators for specific schools or to order performance reports for years after 1993, call Pat McCabe at (916) 657-3740.

ALAMEDA COUNTY HIGH SCHOOL PERFORMANCE VALUES

SCHOOL	A.P.V. VALUE	COMP. GROUP AVG.
STATE-WIDE APV	42.5	
ALAMEDA	54.3	51.5
ALBANY	58.6	56.9
AMADOR VALLEY	57.8	53.9
AMERICAN	46.4	46.7
ARROYO	43.8	43.0
BERKELEY	57.5	55.3
CASTLEMONT	30.6	36.2
CASTRO VALLEY	48.9	49.5
DUBLIN	49.1	45.6
ENCINAL	44.0	44.9
FOOTHILL	52.6	52.0
FREMONT	36.1	36.7
GRANADA	41.2	50.1
HAYWARD	41.2	43.0
IRVINGTON	41.4	44.8
JAMES LOGAN	44.2	45.5
KENNEDY	45.3	46.5
LIVERMORE	46.8	47.3
MCCLYMONDS	34.8	35.8
MISSION SAN JOSE	64.2	56.9
MT. EDEN	44.0	42.5
NEWARK	44.3	43.1
OAKLAND	40.0	36.8
OAKLAND TECH	44.0	37.8
PIEDMONT	73.0	59.0
SAN LEANDRO	47.7	43.9
SAN LORENZO	43.9	39.8
SKYLINE	51.3	46.8
TENNYSON	37.9	38.2
WASHINGTON	53.6	45.9

CONTRA COSTA COUNTY HIGH SCHOOL PERFORMANCE VALUES

SCHOOL	A.P.V. VALUE	COMP. GROUP AVG.
STATE-WIDE	42.5	
ACALANES	67.7	57.9
ALHAMBRA	44.7	47.9
ANTIOCH	42.4	42.9
CALIFORNIA	57.3	54.4
CAMPOLINDO	71.7	58.5
CLAYTON	50.6	53.1
COLLEGE PARK	54.6	49.8
CONCORD	45.4	45.8
DE ANZA	46.2	42.0
EL CERRITO	53.7	45.0
KENNEDY	43.1	37.9
LAS LOMAS	61.3	58.8
LIBERTY	42.3	42.0
MIRAMONTE	75.0	58.9
MONTE VISTA	61.8	57.8
MT. DIABLO	40.1	40.0
NORTHGATE	69.2	58.3
PINOLE VALLEY	52.5	47.7
PITTSBURG	40.5	41.1
RICHMOND	37.6	36.8
SAN RAMON VALLEY	61.0	56.6
SWETT, JOHN	40.5	44.6
YGNACIO VALLEY	51.1	50.6

SAT SCORES

Many four year colleges and universities use the Scholastic Aptitude Test to help them assess the abilities of prospective students. High SAT scores are usually an indication of an affluent, well-educated community; therefore these scores should not be used to judge the effectiveness of individual schools. However, high scores and a large percentage of students taking the test probably indicate that these schools have an academic and social environment that values academic success, a wide range of advanced level classes, and many students who work hard in their classes because they plan to go on to a competitive college.

Beginning with the exams given in 1995, the College Board, which administers the SATs, recentered the scores so that a score of 500 reflects an average score in both the math and verbal section of the exams. Consequently, most scores went up. With recentering, a verbal score of 420 and a math score of 470 under the old scale convert to about 500. To obtain more recent scores, contact the California Department of Education at (916) 657-2273.

AVERAGE SAT SCORES FOR
ALAMEDA COUNTY HIGH SCHOOLS

HIGH SCHOOL	% Of Takers in '94	'94 Verbal	'93 Verbal	'94 Math	'93 Math
NATIONAL	42%	423	424	479	478
STATE-WIDE	46%	413	415	482	484
ALAMEDA	58%	415	395	512	495
ALBANY	70%	428	440	530	563
AMADOR VALLEY	53%	452	457	534	530
AMERICAN	44%	404	400	496	477
ARROYO	41%	376	388	464	461
BERKELEY	66%	475	468	540	548
CASTLEMONT	42%	300	315	365	332
CASTRO VALLEY	46%	448	434	524	514
DUBLIN	54%	409	443	488	517
EMERY	73%	267	352	327	370
ENCINAL	40%	377	429	468	493
FOOTHILL	66%	448	442	521	505
FREMONT	35%	302	288	394	376
GRANADA	44%	437	434	521	520

HIGH SCHOOL	% Of Takers in '94	'94 Verbal	'93Verbal	'94 Math	'93 Math
HAYWARD	36%	403	377	450	437
IRVINGTON (Fremont)	39%	436	405	503	482
JAMES LOGAN (New Haven)	44%	376	378	470	477
KENNEDY (Fremont)	41%	393	401	491	487
LIVERMORE	50%	428	451	509	542
MCCLYMONDS (Oakland)	28%	302	281	343	313
MSN. SAN JOSE (Fremont)	74%	472	468	577	560
MT. EDEN (Hayward)	44%	371	384	456	464
NEWARK	33%	408	410	499	481
OAKLAND	38%	321	333	437	454
OAKLAND TECH	53%	350	346	458	444
PIEDMONT	93%	500	504	589	576
SAN LEANDRO	37%	425	425	503	508
SAN LORENZO	42%	348	384	439	467
SKYLINE (Oakland)	60%	372	399	445	461
TENNYSON (Hayward)	33%	346	356	453	460
WASHINGTON (Fremont)	51%	432	434	518	517

AVERAGE SAT SCORES FOR
CONTRA COSTA COUNTY HIGH SCHOOLS

HIGH SCHOOL	% Of Takers in '94	'94Verbal	'93 Verbal	'94Math	'93 Math
NATIONAL	42%	423	424	479	478
STATE-WIDE	46%	413	415	482	484
ACALANES	78%	505	500	566	561
ALHAMBRA (Martinez)	33%	421	417	509	484
ANTIOCH	36%	405	405	467	453
CALIFORNIA (San Ramon Valley)	57%	438	448	524	514
CAMPOLINDO (Acalanes)	87%	499	489	566	557
CLAYTON (Mt. Diablo)	57%	430	430	514	507
COLLEGE PARK (Mt. Diablo)	54%	442	427	509	514
CONCORD (Mt. Diablo)	34%	416	425	483	471
DE ANZA (Richmond)	48%	374	385	433	464
EL CERRITO (Richmond)	56%	407	409	479	471
KENNEDY (Richmond)	37%	326	373	377	435
LAS LOMAS (Acalanes)	71%	469	469	537	548
LIBERTY	25%	389	391	459	470
MIRAMONTE (Acalanes)	83%	501	520	576	592
MONTE VISTA (San Ramon Valley)	76%	477	473	548	543
MT. DIABLO	35%	364	395	428	462
NORTHGATE (Mt. Diablo)	76%	490	480	569	557
PINOLE VALLEY (Richmond)	53%	399	400	470	484
PITTSBURG	37%	361	373	417	436
RICHMOND	16%	289	294	377	361
SAN RAMON VALLEY	66%	465	466	531	520
SWETT, JOHN	36%	443	453	520	528
YGNACIO VALLEY (MT. DIABLO)	57%	450	444	518	522

Percentage of Students Who Met UC's Subject A Requirement

Freshman entering any branch of the University of California are required to demonstrate proficiency in University-level writing. The requirement can be met by passing the Subject A exam (which is held every May), by achieving a score of 600 or higher on the College Board's English Composition test (the SAT II), or by achieving a score of at least 3 on the AP English exam. This data, compiled by the Office of the President of the University of California, provides information about the graduates of both public and private schools and is one indicator of the strength of a high school's English department and the school's ability to prepare students for college level writing.

GRADUATES OF ALAMEDA COUNTY HIGH SCHOOLS

	TOTAL ADMITTED TO UC			TOTAL ENROLLED IN UC			% WHO MET REQUIREMENTS		
	1992	1993	1994	1992	1993	1994	1992	1993	1994
Total in UC System	30523	32826	34742	19350	20164	20534	62.7%	66.0%	62.5%
High School									
Alameda	43	53	66	30	38	39	60.0%	57.9%	79.5%
Albany	47	49	40	30	38	27	63.3%	71.1%	70.4%
Amador Valley	47	66	40	24	40	27	87.5%	77.5%	88.9%
American	39	31	26	29	18	18	65.5%	66.7%	77.8%
Arroyo	13	24	25	9	19	17	44.4%	73.7%	64.7%
Berkeley	172	176	158	103	108	99	66.0%	78.7%	72.7%
Bishop O'Dowd	133	126	127	94	71	76	77.7%	74.6%	73.7%
Castlemount	6	11	12	4	6	6	0.0%	50.0%	50.0%
Castro Valley	50	55	54	30	33	35	83.3%	69.7%	65.7%
Chinese American	4	4	4	1	1	2	100.0%	0.0%	50.0%
Christian Her.Ac.	0	0	1	0	0	1	n.a.	n.a.	100.0%
Collega Prep	62	61	55	30	25	22	100.0%	100.0%	90.9%
Dublin	18	13	17	12	9	4	66.7%	88.9%	25.0%
Emery	0	0	2	0	0	1	n.a.	n.a.	100.0%
Encinal	20	16	16	13	11	9	69.2%	81.8%	33.3%
Foothill	45	28	41	29	19	25	69.0%	89.5%	80.0%
Fremont (Oakland)	20	31	17	11	21	10	18.2%	28.6%	30.0%
Fremont Christian	5	3	4	1	2	3	100.0%	50.0%	66.7%
Granada	14	19	30	8	7	16	87.5%	85.7%	75.0%

	TOTAL ADMITTED TO UC			TOTAL ENROLLED IN UC			% WHO MET REQUIREMENTS		
	1992	1993	1994	1992	1993	1994	1992	1993	1994
Hayward	28	14	25	12	7	20	75.0%	42.9%	50.0%
Head-Royce	39	32	38	19	10	15	73.7%	90.0%	86.7%
Holy Names	19	25	24	15	18	16	46.7%	61.1%	56.3%
Irvington	16	23	34	6	16	20	33.3%	75.0%	70.0%
James Logan	84	87	84	63	62	50	66.7%	43.5%	56.0%
John F. Kennedy	24	41	29	15	29	15	66.7%	69.0%	66.7%
Livermore	52	61	42	36	37	31	58.3%	81.1%	80.6%
Maybeck	6	5	9	3	3	5	100.0%	100.0%	100.0%
McClymonds	6	5	6	3	4	2	0.0%	25.0%	50.0%
Mission San Jose	119	123	154	86	93	111	77.9%	79.6%	77.5%
Moreau	54	69	61	36	45	36	83.3%	77.8%	63.9%
Mt. Eden	34	39	39	21	21	26	57.1%	52.4%	46.2%
Newark	25	26	34	17	16	19	76.5%	75.0%	73.7%
Oakland	36	43	64	27	33	48	33.3%	27.3%	33.3%
Oakland Tech	49	62	51	35	40	33	28.6%	45.0%	45.5%
Piedmont	58	53	76	31	29	33	64.5%	65.5%	63.6%
Redwood Christn.	6	6	6	3	0	3	100.0%	n.a.	100.0%
St. Elizabeth	8	5	7	3	4	4	0.0%	25.0%	50.0%
St. Jos-Notre Dame	18	19	21	9	13	11	77.8%	69.2%	90.9%
San Leandro	37	34	33	30	24	28	63.3%	83.3%	75.0%
San Lorenzo	13	18	17	8	12	10	75.0%	58.3%	40.0%
Skyline	87	99	93	63	64	57	58.7%	53.1%	49.1%
St Marys College	32	35	33	20	23	20	60.0%	43.5%	45.0%
Tennyson	11	21	17	7	13	9	57.1%	84.6%	33.3%
Valley Christian	4	3	2	4	2	0	50.0%	50.0%	n.a.
Washington	34	47	32	29	35	18	79.3%	62.9%	72.2%

GRADUATES OF CONTRA COSTA
COUNTY HIGH SCHOOLS

	TOTAL ADMITTED TO UC			TOTAL ENROLLED IN UC			% WHO MET REQUIREMENTS		
	1992	1993	1994	1992	1993	1994	1992	1993	1994
Total in UC System	30523	32826	34742	19350	20164	20534	62.7%	66.0%	62.5%
High School									
Acalanes	86	88	94	43	55	54	72.1%	80.0%	74.1%
Alhambra	12	15	15	6	12	9	100.0%	66.7%	66.7%
Antioch	28	24	35	21	12	22	66.7%	75.0%	45.5%
Athenian	15	13	20	5	8	12	80.0%	62.5%	58.3%
Berean Christian	2	4	1	2	2	1	50.0%	100.0%	100.0%
California	36	50	44	24	36	26	75.0%	91.7%	69.2%
Campolindo	84	84	76	53	49	51	69.8%	83.7%	76.5%

	TOTAL ADMITTED TO UC			TOTAL ENROLLED IN UC			% WHO MET REQUIREMENTS		
	1992	1993	1994	1992	1993	1994	1992	1993	1994
Carondelet	47	51	59	35	25	29	74.3%	44.0%	65.5%
Clayton	30	39	29	20	28	20	80.0%	67.9%	80.0%
College Park	31	34	43	18	25	23	66.7%	68.0%	73.9%
Concord	22	25	20	17	16	16	47.1%	56.3%	75.0%
De Anza	34	25	25	21	20	13	42.9%	65.0%	38.5%
De Lasalle	48	56	55	34	34	28	55.9%	58.8%	50.0%
El Cerrito	73	74	57	43	46	41	60.5%	76.1%	73.2%
John Swett	9	11	10	5	10	7	40.0%	70.0%	85.7%
Kennedy	14	16	9	10	13	7	80.0%	53.8%	42.9%
Las Lomas	52	63	80	34	39	48	55.9%	87.2%	79.2%
Liberty	12	18	16	6	10	7	66.7%	90.0%	42.9%
Miramonte	86	100	98	51	58	50	68.6%	82.8%	70.0%
Monte Vista	140	120	110	89	62	62	67.4%	74.2%	67.7%
Mt. Diablo	14	7	18	8	6	15	75.0%	66.7%	46.7%
North Bay Orinda	2	2	1	2	1	1	100.0%	100.0%	0.0%
Northgate	88	98	108	64	62	70	73.4%	77.4%	74.3%
Pinaole Valley	47	69	73	36	46	50	63.9%	56.5%	48.0%
Pittsburg	11	15	21	6	9	14	66.7%	44.4%	78.6%
Richmond	7	7	13	6	7	6	50.0%	28.6%	33.3%
Salesian	6	17	23	5	13	14	40.0%	61.5%	50.0%
San Ramon Valley	96	82	81	60	47	41	73.3%	85.1%	65.9%
Ygnacio Valley	46	48	47	27	34	26	55.6%	82.4%	69.2%

INDEX

St. Barnabas 78
St. Bede 92
St. Benedict 78
St. Bernard 78
St. Catherine of Siena 123
St. Clement 92
St. Columba 78
St. Cornelius 113
St. Cyril 78
St. David 113
St. Edward 92
St. Elizabeth 79
St. Elizabeth High School 107
St. Felicitas 89
St. Francis of Assisi 123
St. Isadore 119
St. Jarlath 79
St. Jerome 113
St. Joachim 89
St. John 89
St. John the Baptist 114
St. Joseph (Alameda) 79
St. Joseph (Fremont) 92
St. Joseph (Pinole) 117
St. Joseph the Worker 71
St. Joseph-Notre Dame High School 107
St. Lawrence O'Toole 79
St. Leander 89
St. Leo's 80
St. Leonard 93
St. Louis Bertrand 80
St. Mary 119
St. Mary's College High School 107
St. Michael's 98
St. Pascal Baylon 80
St. Patrick (Oakland) 80
St. Patrick (Rodeo) 118
St. Paul 114
St. Paul's Episcopal 82
St. Perpetua 119
St. Peter Martyr 126
St. Philip Lutheran 99
St. Philip Neri 80
St. Raymond 98
St. Theresa 80
STARS School 134
Stellar Academy for Dyslexics 111
Subject A exams 165

Sunol Glen School District 58
Sunshine School, The 95

T

Tehiyah Day 115
Trinity Lutheran 120

V

Valley Christian 99
Valley Christian Junior/Senior High 107
Valley Montessori 101
Via Center 111
Vista Christian 115

W

Walden Center and School 76
Walnut Creek Christian Academy 120
Walnut Creek School District 65
West Contra Costa Unified School District 65
Western Association of Schools and Colleges (WASC) 27
Willow Wood School 128
Windrush 117
Woodlands Christian 120
Woodroe Woods School, Inc. 98

Y

Ygnacio Valley Christian 124

Z

Zion Lutheran 83

ORDER FORM FOR PARENTS' GUIDE TO SCHOOL SELECTION

Haskala Press
640 Orange Avenue
Los Altos, CA 94022
(415) 948-4648
FAX: (415) 941-0567

Group Discount Rates (for books sent to same address)
5 - 9 copies	10%
10 - 19 copies	20%
20 or more copies	30%

Shipping: $2.00 for first book, $1.00 for each additional book.
Please send checks only and allow 2-3 weeks.

Please send me:

_____ copies of *Parents' Guide to School Selection in Alameda/Contra Costa County* @ $15.95 each. $ _____

_____ copies of *Parents' Guide to School Selection in San Mateo/Santa Clara County* (1994 ed.) @ $14.95 each. $ _____

Subtract discount (_____%) $ _____

Net Order $ _____

Sales Tax (add 7.75%) $ _____

Shipping $ _____

TOTAL $ _____

Name _____
Address _____
City _____ State _____ Zip _____

NOTES

NOTES

NOTES

NOTES